MEMORABLE MOVIE ROLES

AND THE

Actors Who Played Them

MEMORABLE MOVIE ROLES

AND THE

Actors Who Played Them

Kent Jones

Photographs from the Kobal Collection

CRESCENT BOOKS
New York/Avenel, New Jersey

ISBN 0-517-06964-4

8 7 6 5 4 3 2 1

Memorable Movie Roles and the Actors Who Played Them was prepared and produced by Moore & Moore Publishing, 11 W. 19th Street, New York, New York 10011

Previous pages Charles Chaplin as the Little Tramp in *City Lights*.

These pages (clockwise from upper left) Barbra Streisand as Fanny Brice in *Funny Girl*; Spencer Tracy and Katharine Hepburn as Adam and Amanda Bonner in *Adam's Rib*; Peter O'Toole as T. E. Lawrence in *Lawrence of Arabia*; Lauren Bacall as Marie Browning with co-star Humphrey Bogart in *To Have and Have Not*; Greta Garbo as Marguerite Gautier in *Camille*; Michael Douglas as Gordon Gecko in *Wall Street*; and Gene Kelly as Don Lockwood in *Singin' in the Rain*.

AN M&M BOOK

Project Director & Editor Gary Fishgall

Editorial Assistants Maxine Dormer, Ben D'Amprisi, Jr.

Copy Editing Keith Walsh

Photo Editor Bob Cosenza

Designer Marcy Stamper

Separations and Printing Regent Publishing Services Ltd.

$\mathcal{C}$ontents

What constitutes a memorable movie role? Of course there are no hard and fast rules, but the question lingers in the same way that, in the back of our minds, we think that somewhere there exists a definition of love. Like the unfathomable passion between a man and a woman, no one can say what makes a movie role memorable, but one knows it when one sees it.

It would seem that a memorable movie role would be somewhat less ephemeral than romance. Somehow, one thinks, it should be re-ducible to its nuts-and-bolts essence, perhaps made formulaic. If one gives the right script to the right director and gives that director the right actor in the right role, then one apparently has it made. If this were only true, Hollywood would be Utopia, and the money would come pouring into its coffers in a never-ending stream. But how many movie projects have been launched by seemingly golden combinations of talent only to end with lackluster results, films that never quite hit the mark?

For every apparent rule, there is an excep-

ABOVE: *William Holden and Gloria Swanson as Joe Gillis and Norma Desmond in* Sunset Boulevard.

tion. For instance, one might be tempted to say that an actor's most memorable role is that which first thrust him or her into the public eye. Surely that was the case with James Cagney in *The Public Enemy* and Dustin Hoffman in *The Graduate*. But sometimes a performer comes across a role in mid- or late career that seems to sum up the qualities with which he or she is associated—as with Bette Davis in *All About Eve* and John Wayne in *The Searchers*. In still other instances, a role is memorable for allowing us to see an actor in a new way. In *Mildred Pierce,* for example, Joan Crawford traded in her image as a carefully coiffed MGM siren for that of a plainer, less polished woman and gave a badly needed boost to her then-sagging career. On the other hand sometimes a performance is so memorable that the actor who plays it—Bela Lugosi as Dracula, Anthony Perkins as Norman Bates—can't seem to find other roles that measure up and he or she becomes trapped by the very creation that was so inspired.

Of course, in some instances great performances don't imprint themselves on the moviegoing public's consciousness because the role as written doesn't amount to much. And yet, what about a character like Vivian Ward, the charming prostitute, in *Pretty Woman*? By any reasonable standard, Vivian is an impossibility—a sweet, pretty, well-rounded young woman who happens to be making a living as a Los Angeles hooker. Not even a call girl, mind you, but a streetwalker. And plausibility aside—because, as all experienced moviegoers know, plausibility has next to nothing to do with what makes a good movie—it is a thinly written part. But Julia Roberts brought a sweet, springtime charm to the role, Richard Gere's Edward Lewis was a suavely willing foil, and director Garry Marshall had a fine, graceful touch. And last but not least, in the summer of 1990, the public was waiting with open arms for a *Pretty Woman*. That is a crucial element. Marshall's follow-up, *Frankie and Johnny,* was another romance, with other distinguished actors (Michelle Pfeiffer and Al Pacino) based on a wonderful play by Terrence McNally. But as good as the film and its stars were, it just didn't catch fire with the public.

Characters can be memorable because they undergo particular experiences or changes with which an audience identifies or for which it yearns, as was the case with Julia Roberts' Vivian. But they can also linger in the mind because they embody cultural change, as was the case with Jill Clayburgh's Erika in *An Unmarried Woman,* or they have a humorous cathartic effect. Who, for instance, has not recognized in the outrageous bumblings of Peter Sellers' Inspector Clouseau one's own slips of the tongue or faux pas?

In order to be memorable, a movie role doesn't even require good acting. Even though the movies were still in their relative infancy in 1921, when Rudolph Valentino made *The*

Sheik, it seems unlikely that his legions of fans would have described the florid, wild gesturing they were watching as great (or even passable) acting. Johnny Weissmuller was the first to admit that he really couldn't act, but anyone who has ever seen him as Tarzan knows that he was the right man for the job. What Gary Cooper or Marlene Dietrich did on screen in *Meet John Doe* and *Shanghai Express,* respectively, may not have been great acting, but it was certainly eloquent and riveting.

And for the actors who *can* act, their most memorable roles may not even be their best—far from it, in some cases. Burt Reynolds himself would probably list over two-thirds of his movie roles in descending order of quality before he would get to *Smokey and the Bandit.* *Deliverance* would probably be at the top, and there is no question that his performance in that film is the superior piece of work. But it was as the carefree bootlegger in the 1977 chase picture that Reynolds reached the peak of his popular appeal. As the Bandit, he connected with people by meeting them at eye level rather than from the slightly higher aesthetic perch of *Deliverance.*

Steve McQueen is another case in point. He was a good, if rather limited, actor in movies like *Baby, the Rain Must Fall* and *The Cincinnati Kid,* but he made his name with a series of almost somnambulant appearances in modish action films like *The Thomas Crown Affair* and *Bullitt.* *Bullitt* is remembered now for its death-defying high-speed car chase through the streets of San Francisco, and Mc-Queen seems almost like a blur in it, so expressionless and silent does he remain throughout

much of the film. But in his day, that silence represented inscrutable cool to a younger generation of moviegoers. The public was there to meet McQueen in 1968, just like it would be waiting for Julia Roberts 22 years later.

Of course being a great actor does not guarantee that one will at some point play a memorable movie role. Laurence Olivier, who is often held up as an example of what constitutes great acting, is a case in point. He gave many mesmerizing performances throughout his film career but none seems to have the spark struck elsewhere by lesser talents.

Of course, that is just my opinion. Others may disagree. It is important to acknowledge the subjective element at work in this book; not only in terms of who was chosen for inclusion but, in some cases, what role was chosen. One could certainly argue, for example, that Jack Nicholson should have been represented by *Five Easy Pieces* or Paul Newman by *Hud* or Sophia Loren by *Two Women* instead of *One Flew Over the Cuckoo's Nest, The Hustler,* and *Marriage, Italian Style,* respectively.

Still, upon reflection, perhaps there is something more to the analogy of love and its elusive definition and the essence of the memorable movie role. Perhaps falling in love and recognizing a memorable movie role are one and the same. Because on those occasions when all the fragile elements that make up the miracle of film meet the equally fragile elements of film-watching and the result ignites to form an alchemical compound, like James Stewart in *Mr. Smith Goes to Washington* or Spencer Tracy and Katharine Hepburn in *Adam's Rib,* it really is love. Love at first sight, that is. ❧

MEMORABLE MOVIE ROLES

❧ AND THE ❧

Actors Who Played Them

Mr. *Smith Goes to Washington* was meant for Gary Cooper. He had starred in the first film of director Frank Capra's populist trilogy, *Mr. Deeds Goes to Town* (1936), and seemed perfect for Jefferson Smith, the political naïf who is appointed to a vacant seat in the U.S. Senate where, against all odds, he destroys his party's corrupt machine. But Capra decided that Cooper was not right after all. The character cried out for a passion that

the stoic actor could not deliver. He chose instead a rising youngster named James Stewart, who had starred in Capra's adaptation of George S. Kaufman and Moss Hart's play, *You Can't Take It With You*, the year before.

The depth of feeling that runs through Stewart's performance in this film is immensely moving and almost embarrassing in its intimacy. He was a tall, gangly, unseasoned performer playing a character of like kind. When Jeff visits the Lincoln Memorial, one can almost feel

the lump in his throat. And for his impassioned filibuster scenes

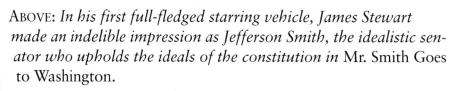

ABOVE: *In his first full-fledged starring vehicle, James Stewart made an indelible impression as Jefferson Smith, the idealistic senator who upholds the ideals of the constitution in* Mr. Smith Goes to Washington.

LEFT: *Stewart is seen here in one of his later, more disturbing, roles as a father in search of his kidnapped son in Alfred Hitchcock's* The Man Who Knew Too Much *(1956).*

at the film's end, Stewart took his character (and his vocal chords, which Capra had coated with mercury to produce a hoarse, rasping effect) to a dangerous, neurotic edge to which he would return only in his later films, particularly those directed by Alfred Hitchcock. His trademark stutter and open-mouthed awe were more or less born with *Mr. Smith*, the first full-fledged vehicle for one of Hollywood's greatest actors.

ABOVE: *Stewart brought his all-American, idealistic charm to the role of big band leader Glenn Miller in the 1954 bio-pic,* The Glenn Miller Story.

BELOW: *Stewart worked for the second and last time with director Frank Capra in* It's A Wonderful Life *(1946), the actor's favorite of his films. He played George Bailey, an ordinary man who gets to see what life would be like if he had never been born. Here George is surrounded by family and friends, including his Uncle Billy (Thomas Mitchell) and his wife, Mary (Donna Reed).*

Mr. Smith Goes to Washington
(1939)
Screenplay by Sidney Buchman. Produced and directed by Frank Capra.
(Columbia) 130 m.

⇜ TOP GUN ⇝

I t is interesting now to go back and look at director Francis Ford Coppola's 1982 film *The Outsiders*. One can see most of what would soon come to be known as the Brat Pack peppered throughout the movie in roles of various sizes. These actors were at the beginnings of their careers, and it was impossible to predict who would become leading men and who would

Top Gun
(1986)
Screenplay by Jim Cash and Jack Epps, Jr.
Produced by Don Simpson and Jerry Bruckheimer.
Directed by Tony Scott.
(Paramount) 110 m.

fall by the wayside. Tom Cruise, his trademark smile shining from under a face covered with dirt and axle grease, was in there in a relatively small role. That smile would become a key to his emergence as a superstar as well as an integral part of his 1986 breakthrough, *Top Gun*.

Cruise was the only Brat Packer to achieve mega-stardom, with the possible exception of Patrick Swayze, who was also seen in *The Outsiders*. Unlike many of his fellow young actors, Cruise has a genuine

nice-guy warmth and radiates sincerity. He has certainly had richer roles, most notably in *The Color of Money* (1987) and *Born On the Fourth of July* (1990), but it was the sleek 1986 film about navy jet pilots, following in the wake of *Risky Business* (1983), that put him over the top.

Top Gun makes no bones about being a character study: it is built for speed, as close to an amusement park ride as a film can get, covered with attractive trimmings including a nonstop rock score, colorful sunsets, pseudo tough-guy dialogue, and some hot love scenes between Cruise and his co-star, Kelly McGillis. Dramatically, the film, which charts the humanization of a cocky flyer who wants to be "the best in the world," is minimal at best, but it is an ample showcase for Cruise's disarming charm—his character flashes his grin like a tough guy flashes a switchblade.

Following up on his success in 1983's Risky Business, *Brat Packer Tom Cruise became a superstar playing the cocky navy pilot known by the code name Maverick in* Top Gun.

SHE DONE HIM WRONG

Although Mae West was 40 years old by the time she sauntered into the movies, it was said that she stole everything but the cameras on her first film, Night After Night (1932). Paramount, knowing that it had something in the former vaudeville star, based her next movie on her own play, Diamond Lil, about a Gay Nineties saloon singer mixed up with a batch of unsavory men. She Done Him Wrong was West at her most undiluted, raciest best.

West was not beautiful by any stretch of the imagination. Her appeal lay in her frankness and her characters' obvious enjoyment of sex. The famous swagger was always a prelude to an encounter with some hunk or other, greeted with a suggestive bon mot in her inevitably husky voice. When, for example, in She Done Him Wrong, a very young Cary Grant's undercover cop tries to slip handcuffs on her, she says, "Are those things necessary? I wasn't born with them, you know." The cop replies, "A lot of men would be better off if you had," to which Lou retorts, "Well, you know, hands aren't everything." At the end of her first meeting with the cop, she gives him the once over and says, simply, "You can be had."

Unfortunately for West, her reign as sex queen of the movies was short-lived. When the production code, a strict form of built-in censorship, was inaugurated in 1934, the movies lost much of their raciness. West's films thereafter became far less insinuating and her screen persona suffered for it. She was no longer allowed to have moments like the one in She Done Him Wrong where every prisoner in a cellblock greets Lou with a special romantic remembrance as she goes to see an old boyfriend, nor could she sing songs with lines like "Even though I'm a fast woman/I like a man who takes his time."

Mae West sizes up a potential victim as Diamond Lil, Queen of the Gay 90s, in She Done Him Wrong.

She Done Him Wrong
(1933)
Screenplay by
Harvey Thew and
John Bright, based on the
play *Diamond Lil*
by Mae West.
Directed by
Lowell Sherman.
(Paramount) 66 m.

Orphaned at the age of five, Barbara Stanwyck became independent when very young, making her way into show business as a dancer and starting to work in films in the late 1920s. She was one of the few stars of her generation who did not sign with a specific studio, choosing instead to remain a free agent throughout her career. This spirit of independence informed her acting as well as her life—she always seemed like a self-possessed individual no matter what role she played. Her confidence was certainly a key ingredient in her portrayal of the treacherous Phyllis Dietrichson

Barbara Stanwyck created the prototypical hard-boiled femme fatale with her portrayal of Phyllis Dietrichson in the film version of James M. Cain's Double Indemnity.

in *Double Indemnity*.

With bleached blond hair, tight sweaters, and a fetching ankle bracelet, Phyllis lures a cynical insurance agent named Walter Neff (Fred MacMurray) into helping her murder her husband and cash in his life insurance policy (James M. Cain based the character in the original novel on the real-life 1920s case of Ruth Snyder). Stanwyck's performance expertly captured Phyllis' boredom, her shallow disregard for any-thing but material goods, and her passionate desire to be free of all constraints. And Stanwyck's unusual looks—critic Manny Farber once described her as having a "Roman nose"—gave her character added poignancy. Lacking natural beauty, Phyllis puts all her energies into her appearance. She works to be sexy. When the term *femme fatale* comes up in movie history, its prototype can be found here, in Stanwyck's treacherous hausfrau. Kathleen Turner's character in *Body Heat* (1981), for instance, is almost a carbon copy.

*Although she is perhaps best remembered as a dramatic actress, Barbara Stanwyck appeared in quite a few comedies in the 1940s. Among the most notable of these was Preston Sturges' *The Lady Eve *(1941), in which she played a con-artist in love with a bumbling millionaire played by Henry Fonda.*

Double Indemnity
(1944)
Screenplay by Billy Wilder and Raymond Chandler, based on the novel by James M. Cain.
Produced by Joseph Sistrom.
Directed by Billy Wilder.
(Paramount) 106 m.

Sean Connery was an almost unknown Scottish actor when he was chosen for the role of Ian Fleming's James Bond by producer Albert R. Broccoli, known to his friends as Cubby. Patrick McGoohan, who went on to star in the popular TV series *Secret Agent* and *The Prisoner,* and Roger Moore, who would take over as Bond in 1973 after Connery became sick of the role, were also candidates. (Fleming himself pictured the role differently: his ideal casting for Bond was Hoagy Carmichael.)

Once he had signed on, Connery went to work with a speech coach to refine his accent a bit, and he learned from director Terence Young the sophisticated manner that was 007's trademark. His efforts paid off, for in the film he struck a perfect balance between the deadly roughneck with a "license to

Connery won an Oscar for his late-career role as the wizened, tough Chicago cop who tries to help Elliot Ness (Kevin Costner) catch Al Capone in The Untouchables *(1987).*

kill" and the posh gentleman.

The first, nearly gadget-free film of the long series takes Bond to Jamaica to do battle with the evil Dr. No (Joseph Wiseman), who has a nuclear arsenal positioned on a small island nearby. At this early stage of the series, Bond's complete self-confidence had not become the object of such arch humor. However, he still has time to bed three women, including one enemy agent and Honey Ryder (Ursula Andress), whom he finds innocently searching for shells on Dr. No's beach. As the series progressed, the scenic adventurism, the brazen sexuality (represented by a parade of beautiful, curvaceous women), the hi-tech gadgetry, and the outrageous vil-

Dr. No
(1962)

Screenplay by Richard Maibaum, Johanna Harwood, and Berkley Mather, based on the novel by Ian Fleming. Produced by Harry Saltzman and Albert R. Broccoli. Directed by Terence Young.

(United Artists) 111 m.

Connery is seen here in one of his finest post-007 roles, as the British army officer and adventurer in director John Huston's adaptation of Rudyard Kipling's The Man Who Would Be King *(1975).*

lains (Gert Frobe's Goldfinger being perhaps the prototype) became trademarks. But Connery plied his trade throughout his five stints (six if one counts his mellow 1983 return in the independent *Thunderball* remake, *Never Say Never Again*) with good humor, panache, cool confidence, and a refined brutality that had a chilling effect whenever it appeared.

Little-known Scottish actor Sean Connery became famous the world over as James Bond, the British secret agent with a license to kill. Dr. No marked the first of his six appearances as Ian Fleming's hero.

TO HAVE AND HAVE NOT

Before she was Lauren Bacall and Bogie's baby, she was Betty Joan Persky, an East Coast model signed by independent director-producer Howard Hawks. To prepare her for her first screen appearance, Hawks sent her off to get her voice from a nasal squeak to the low, throaty drawl filmgoers know and love. Then she made her debut at 19, in Hawks' loose adaptation of the Hemingway novel, *To Have and Have Not.* Hawks and his writers (including novelist William Faulkner) fashioned for her the part of the tough, wayfaring Marie on the theory that she could be as insolent on screen as Bogart. Were they ever right.

If Bacall's acting was a bit unsure at moments, in this, her first outing, her sinuous walk, feline features, and calculated cool more than made up for it. Bogart wasn't the only one who fell in love; she was instantly popular. As critic James Agee wrote, "She managed to get across the toughest girl a piously regenerate Hollywood has dreamed of in a long, long while."

To Have and Have Not
(1944)
Screenplay by Jules Furthman and William Faulkner, based on the novel by Ernest Hemingway. Produced and directed by Howard Hawks. (Warner Bros.) 100 m.

Bacall had many terrific moments in the movie: the scene in which Marie doesn't even flinch when she is slapped across the face by a Vichy police captain (Dan Seymour), played with deadpan aplomb; and of course the intimate love scenes with Bogart's Harry (or Steve, as Marie calls him for some unexplained reason), culminating in her supremely confident reading of one of the most famous lines in film history: "You know how to whistle, don't you? You just put your lips together and . . . blow."

LEFT: *Bacall's sinuous walk, feline features, and calculated cool found a home in director Vincente Minnelli's comedy,* Designing Woman *(1957).*

OPPOSITE: *Lauren Bacall was only 19 years old when she made her debut as the no-nonsense girl, Marie, and fell in love with her co-star, Humphrey Bogart, in the adaptation of Ernest Hemingway's* To Have and Have Not.

BONNIE AND CLYDE

Over the years, Warren Beatty has become something more than an actor. He is now a sort of merchant of his own image, parcelling it out every so often in carefully chosen vehicles that he often produces as well. His first venture behind the camera was a film that uncannily caught the anarchic mood of the country at the time. And for his co-star, he cast a beautiful young stage actress who had made her film debut earlier that year in *The Happening* (1967).

Bonnie and Clyde
(1967)
Screenplay by
Robert Benton an
David Newman.
Produced by
Warren Beatty.
Directed by Arthur Penn.
(Warner Bros.) 111 m.

The rebellious American youths of the 1960s could certainly identify with Clyde Barrow and Bonnie Parker as played by Warren Beatty and Faye Dunaway in Bonnie and Clyde.

Anyone who has ever seen photos of the real Bonnie and Clyde knows that Beatty and director Arthur Penn (a second choice after French director Francois Truffaut dropped out) weren't after surface realism. Faye Dunaway, on her worst day, is still miles off from the genuine plug-ugly 1930s desperado. But she and Beatty made a poignant couple: he played the role with stuttering shyness, accentuating his character's impotence; she played Bonnie with reckless abandon, ruthless for exhilaration. The rebellious American youths of the day could certainly identify with them. Indeed, the film's immortal tag line, "They're young. . . they're in love. . . and they kill people," suggested that the beautiful Bonnie and Clyde were really just a couple of kids, out for some dangerous fun. As Clyde sees it, "Things just got out of hand," or so he asserts after he kills his first victim, almost angry at the man for forcing him to resort to such an extreme.

The scenes of violence, and particularly the bloody massacre at the end, were upsetting at the time and remain so today because of the otherwise light-hearted film's sudden eruptions into graphic bloodletting. And although Bonnie and Clyde kill people, the audience's sympathies are with them. As director Martin Scorsese put it, "They wore the best clothes."

⊰ DEATH WISH ⊱

Charles Bronson's Paul Kersey was the second great screen vigilante of his day, preceded by three years by Clint Eastwood's Harry Callahan in *Dirty Harry* (1971). Both films provoked a flurry of social commentary—they were thought to promote vigilantism and, depending upon how one felt about the law-and-order issue, were praised or scorned. Of the two films, *Death Wish* probably came closer to hitting a raw nerve with the public. For Callahan at least was a law enforcement officer who takes the law into his own hands in order to uphold it, whereas Kersey was a cultured Manhattan architect out to avenge the murder of his wife and the rape of his daughter by a gang of thugs. Bronson's Slavic face, with its slit eyes and weathered skin, generally appears inscrutable, a quality well-suited to a man who houses such unfathomable pain that he feels compelled to seek out and kill the city's lowlifes.

Bronson was none too convincing as an architect, however. His look and overall affect is decidedly blue collar. But the film spent little time worrying about Paul Kersey's career. It was best used as a plot device for giving the gun-shy urbanite a pistol, which came to him as a gift from a grateful client (Stuart Margolin). Still, however, it was the character's white collar background that distinguished him. He did not feel the sort of smug satisfaction after a killing that has become so common to screen vigilantes. In fact, after dispatching his first group of muggers, he goes home and vomits.

Although he doesn't exactly wallow in guilt over his violent forays, neither does he gloat or jump for joy—he remains passive, mysterious.

Bronson was questioned about the political motives of those making the film, and, with a straightforwardness that might have come from Kersey himself, said that they were only out to produce a good thriller.

Death Wish
(1974)
Screenplay by
Wendell Mayes, based on
the novel by Brian Garfield.
Produced by Hal Landers,
Bobby Roberts, and
Michael Winner. Directed
by Michael Winner.
(Paramount) 94 m.

Many Americans were shocked by the image of a cultured Manhattan architect prowling the streets of New York killing off the city's lowlifes. Soft-spoken, inscrutable Charles Bronson assayed the role in Death Wish *and its two sequels.*

MEET JOHN DOE

Meet John Doe
(1941)
Screenplay by Robert
Riskin, based on the story
"The Life and Death of John
Doe" by Richard Connell
and Robert Presnell.
Produced and directed by
Frank Capra.
(Columbia) 132 m.

When director Frank Capra decided to film the third part of what has come to be known as his populist trilogy from a short story by Richard Connell and Robert Presnell called "The Life and Death of John Doe," he had no doubt about whom he wanted to play the lead. When Gary Cooper was asked, a script was not yet ready, but the actor signed on sight unseen. He and Capra had worked together harmoniously and to great acclaim four years earlier in the first part of the trilogy, *Mr. Deeds Goes To Town* (1936). Cooper had also been considered for *Mr. Smith Goes To Washington* (1939), the middle of the three films, but in that instance the director decided that he needed someone a little more fiery for the lead and chose James Stewart. Cooper, however, was well-suited for the role of John Doe, the hobo recruited by an ambitious newspaperwoman (Barbara Stanwyck) to commit suicide on New Year's Eve on behalf of all the poor of America.

By 1940, when the film was made, Cooper's extraordinary features had acquired a touch of cragginess. In fact, he looked as though he could join the

Cooper's first picture with Frank Capra, his director on Meet John Doe, *was* Mr. Deeds Goes To Town *(1936). In it the actor played a small-town poet who moves to New York after inheriting a fortune.*

BELOW: *Cooper's plain, unaffected style was just right for the role of Alvin York, the World War I hero who put his pacifist beliefs aside and used his abilities as an expert marksman. Cooper won an Oscar for work on* Sergeant York *(1941).*

Cooper won his second Oscar playing Will Kane, the sheriff who faces a band of outlaws alone in the 1952 Western, High Noon.

American presidents on Mount Rushmore. Moreover, in contrast to the brasher stars of the day—Gable, Tracy, Cagney, and Bogart—he projected a childlike intransigence and faith in human nature that made him entirely credible as an average man who becomes a hero because of his basic goodness. Capra had many problems with the denouement of the film and shot multiple versions. Perhaps, in the end, he still failed to find a satisfactory resolution, but Cooper's delivery of

John Doe's final apology to his duped fans, delivered in the actor's plain, unaffected style, is moving nevertheless. It was perhaps the cinema's most effective use of this minimalist actor whose stoic presence was his greatest, most eloquent tool.

Gary Cooper plays John Doe, a common man turned into a national symbol by a newspaper reporter and editor (Barbara Stanwyck and James Gleason) in Frank Capra's Meet John Doe.

Christopher Reeve was a relatively unknown Juilliard graduate when he was cast by executive producer Alexander Salkind in his enormously expensive version of the classic comic strip. Salkind decided on an unknown after considering a long list of major stars, including Clint Eastwood, Charles Bronson, and Burt Reynolds! It was a gamble that paid off. The four installments of the *Superman* series, for all their special effects and all-star casts, owe much of their success and conviction to Reeve, who inhabited the role from his first moment on-screen. He was so right, in fact, that his skill and wit weren't sufficiently appreciated at the time.

Unlike many novices thrown into the cinematic spotlight, Reeve showed great confidence from the outset. With his square-jawed, all-American

Reeve is pictured here as the bumbling Clark Kent, a side of his role as Superman that allowed him to amply display his comic talent. Here he is being rebuffed by fellow Daily Planet reporter Lois Lane (Margot Kidder).

Superman: The Movie
(1978)
Screenplay by Mario Puzo, David Newman, Leslie Newman, and Robert Benton, based on a story by Puzo, from the comic strip created by Jerry Siegel and Joel Shuster. Produced by Pierre Spengler. Directed by Richard Donner.
(Warner Bros.) 142 m.

handsomeness, muscular physique (which he trained hard to get), and smoothly reassuring voice, he certainly seemed right as the Man of Steel. But it was his bumbling Clark Kent, in sync with the film's tongue-in-cheek approach, that showed his skill as a comic actor.

Reeve hasn't fared so well in other roles, perhaps because he became so closely identified with this one. Although he was good in *The Bostonians* (1984) and *Switching Channels* (1988), there was always the sneaking suspicion that he would run to the nearest phone booth, change into his costume, and fly away.

OPPOSITE: *Surrounded by an all-star cast, Christopher Reeve made an impressive film debut as the Man of Steel in the extravaganza* Superman: The Movie.

Joan Bennett. Jean Arthur. Paulette Goddard. Bette Davis. Lana Turner. These were among the hundreds of actresses in the running for the role of all roles: Scarlett O'Hara, the fierce, prideful flower of Southern womanhood who fights to save her beloved homestead, Tara, in the devastating aftermath of the Civil War. Producer David O. Selznick engineered a nationwide search to cast the treasured role of the heroine of Margaret Mitchell's *Gone With the Wind*. After all the hoopla, he was introduced to the British actress he would cast after filming had begun (it was during the shooting of

Producer David O. Selznick auditioned hundreds of actresses, both famous and unknown, before he cast classically trained British actress Vivien Leigh as Scarlett. She won her first Oscar for the role.

the burning of Atlanta sequence, to be exact) by his brother, agent Myron Selznick.

Mitchell begins her novel with the words, "Scarlett O'Hara was not beautiful . . . ," and right off the bat Selznick violated his source. In gorgeous Technicolor, Vivien Leigh was ravishing, but her lofty manner and bright alertness perfectly fit the author's conception of an impetuous, spoiled Southern belle. As for Rhett Butler, the self-assured pragmatist, so un-

THE WIND ✑

Since Gone With the Wind *premiered in 1939, moviegoers have remained captivated by the tempestuous relationship between a feisty Southern belle named Scarlett (Vivien Leigh), and a straight-talking cad named Rhett (Clark Gable). Here the newly widowed Scarlett allows Rhett to talk her into dancing at a fund-raising event.*

like the courtly cavaliers surrounding Scarlett, there was never any doubt about who should play that role. Selznick wrangled to get Clark Gable on loan from MGM, even though the "King of Holly-wood" wasn't all that eager to play the part of the cad with a heart of gold. But the public insisted on him and in this case the public knew best: the role fit Gable like a glove. The famous movie star and the classically trained newcomer matched one another in cockiness and assured presence. Their Scarlett and Rhett are perfectly matched in their iron-willed struggle between love and contempt for one another, and the disparity in Leigh's and Gable's backgrounds as actors added an extra dimension to their performances. Their star-power dominated this titanic film, and made it the classic that it remains today.

The public demanded that Clark Gable, at that time known as the "King of Hollywood," play the pragmatic businessman Rhett Butler.

⊳⊳⊳⊳⊳⊳⊳⊳⊳⊳⊳⊳⊳

Gone With the Wind
(1939)
Screenplay by Sidney
Howard, based on the novel
by Margaret Mitchell.
Produced by
David O. Selznick.
Directed by Victor Fleming.
(MGM) 220 m.

---◦◼◦---

THE HOUND OF THE BASKERVILLES

When producer Darryl F. Zanuck decided to do a screen version of Sir Arthur Conan Doyle's *The Hound of the Baskervilles,* he followed the advice of a chance remark at a party and cast the British character actor Basil Rathbone as detective Sherlock Holmes. Rathbone's hawk-like nose and tall, angular physique combined with his intensity and clipped British accent to make him perfect for the role of Doyle's brilliant master detective. And to think that one of the most famous film series of all time was launched by a capricious comment at a Hollywood soiree.

Rathbone and Nigel Bruce (who played Dr. Watson as a fool and comic foil, not at all in the spirit of the quiet, steady Doyle

character), repeated their roles in 13 sequels throughout the early 1940s. *Baskervilles* and its immediate successor, *The Adventures of Sherlock Holmes* (1939), were the best of the series, both beautiful period pieces.

The Hound of the Baskervilles
(1939)
Screenplay by Ernest Pascal, based on the novel by Sir Arthur Conan Doyle. Produced by Gene Markey. Directed by Sidney Lanfield.
(20th Century Fox) 85 m.

Baskervilles, which ends with the line, "Quick, Watson—the needle!" even preserves Holmes' cocaine addiction. The ensuing modern-dress sequels, B-movies with a patriotic wartime spirit, are engaging only thanks to the byplay of Bruce and Rathbone. For anyone who has read any of the Sherlock Holmes stories, the effect of seeing Rathbone in the first two offerings, decked out in tweed cape and hat, magnifying glass in hand, beady eyes riveted to a clue that no one else can see, is eerily like seeing a character step right off the printed page.

To many, Basil Rathbone was the very image of Sherlock Holmes come to life. He is seen here in The Adventures of Sherlock Holmes, *the second in the series of films in which he played the world's greatest detective.*

The legend goes that Katharine Hepburn, Garson Kanin, and Ruth Gordon conspired to create a sizable role for Judy Holliday in *Adam's Rib* (1949) in order to convince Columbia boss Harry Cohn to let her repeat her Broadway success in the film version of Kanin's play, *Born Yesterday*. The efforts of this little band worked and Holliday walked off with the 1950 Oscar for Best Actress in her first starring role.

Not that she didn't have good material to work from. The magic of Kanin's character lies in her transformation. But unlike Shaw's *Pygmalion,* the change is more inward than outward. Billie is the paramour of a crooked Washington junk dealer named Harry Brock (Broderick Crawford), a dictatorial loudmouth who treats her like a trophy he's won—to him she's a dumb blonde and he wants to keep her that way. He just wants to polish her up a bit, so when he hires a reporter named Paul Verral (William Holden) to tutor her, he doesn't count on her self-actualization and in-

In the film adaptation of Garson Kanin's Born Yesterday, *Judy Holliday re-created her smash-hit stage performance as Billie Dawn, the "dumb" kept woman who blossoms under the tutelage of reporter Paul Verrall (William Holden). The actress won an Oscar for this, her first starring role.*

creasing sense of self-worth. As she falls in love with Paul, she realizes that she isn't as dumb as she thinks she is.

Director George Cukor said that Holliday was the most exacting actress he worked with—"If there was a comma in the text, you

Born Yesterday
(1950)
Screenplay by Albert Mannheimer, based on the play by Garson Kanin. Produced by S. Sylvan Simon. Directed by George Cukor.
(Columbia) 103 m.

would hear it when she spoke the line." The precise inflections of the nasal New York falsetto she effected for the role reached a comic peak during the famous card game sequence, in which she repeatedly bests her increasingly furious boyfriend. As she blithely lays down the winning hand, her pronunciation of the word "gin"—a combination of triumph and nonchalance—is unforgettable.

With teeth bared and jaw thrust forward, Kirk Douglas' Spartacus, leader of a slave revolt in ancient Rome, is what one today might call a nonverbal individual. As he trains to become a gladiator and learns to risk death every time he steps into the ring for the entertainment of his patrician masters, he is like a ball of pure energy waiting to explode, suffering all the torture and humiliation heaped upon him with stoic endurance. Douglas never used his hard, sinewy physique to better effect than in this epic. The body that had been trained for the sport of others becomes the very symbol of his character's deep resentment. And when he does finally lead his fellow combatants in an escape from the gladiatorial school and that chance act of defiance spearheads into a massive revolt, Spartacus' joy bursts out

The intensity that Kirk Douglas brought to the title role in Spartacus *can be seen in this photo, in which he prepares to lead his slave army against the might of the Roman empire. Douglas also produced the epic.*

shooting started (Anthony Mann) and hired a young Stanley Kubrick, with whom he also disagreed fiercely. That Douglas believed in the project is certainly evident from his performance. He invested Spartacus with such emotion that when one is watching the film, the temptation is great to stand up to the Roman centurions as they seek to identify the leader of the revolt and join the slaves in declaring, one by one: "I'm Spartacus!"

> **Spartacus**
> (1960)
> Screenplay by Dalton Trumbo, based on the novel by Howard Fast. Produced by Edward Lewis. Executive Producer, Kirk Douglas. Directed by Stanley Kubrick
> (Universal) 196 m.

Three years after making his film debut, Douglas emerged as a major star, playing Midge, the cocky, forceful boxer in Champion *(1949).*

in speech. Douglas brought such intensity to the role that it seemed as if he really could have inspired a band of outlaws to take on 50 Roman legions. The revolt was Spartacus' triumph. The film was Douglas'.

Perhaps the success of *Spartacus* was all the more fitting then, because it was Kirk Douglas' own project. In an age when few actors developed their own properties, he nurtured and pro-

duced it himself, with the same conviction and forbearance as his character. He worked hard to get the actors he wanted, even going so far as to have different versions of the script written, favoring the role of the individual to whom it was being sent. He fired one director after

In 1956, Douglas departed from the brash, physically powerful characters he usually played to portray the lonely, anguished artist, Vincent van Gogh, in Lust for Life. *But the usual Douglas intensity was used to great effect in the film.*

ALL ABOUT EVE

The role of Margo Channing in *All About Eve* seems to belong completely, totally, and forever to Bette Davis. Her Margo, a grand dame of the theater with a temperament to match her enormous talent, is such an even match for Davis' own public persona that another actress in the part is unthinkable. This is a true testament to Davis,

Bette Davis, pictured here with Henry Fonda, won her second Oscar in three years for her performance in the 1938 southern drama Jezebel.

Davis fought for her independence in her early years as a star so that she could play the parts she wanted. Here she is pictured with co-star Leslie Howard in her first major role, the slangy Cockney waitress in the 1934 adaptation of Somerset Maugham's Of Human Bondage.

because Margo, the signature role of her long career, was written for Claudette Colbert. Not only was it not intended for Davis, she was a last-minute replacement.

Davis, who stood up to all the studio bosses early in her career and fought for her independence within the movie industry, was perfect as the actress who rules Broadway. And it seems so right that the perennial ugly duckling of the movies play a woman unseated at the peak of

her fame by a young, beautiful ingenue, Eve Harrington (Anne Baxter, originally cast because of her likeness to Colbert in profile). In a film bristling with sharp-witted and acid-tongued characters (including theater critic Addison DeWitt, played by the epitome of bored sophistication, George Sanders), Davis' Margo rules like a queen, the sharpest and the most acerbic of them all. Yet the character's vulnerability came through as well, with Davis masterfully showing the

LEFT: *Unlike most actresses of her generation, who were extremely self-conscious about their appearance on screen, Davis was even willing to shave her hairline for her portrayal of Queen Elizabeth I in* The Virgin Queen *(1955). She had also played the monarch in* The Private Lives of Elizabeth and Essex *(1939).*

All About Eve
(1950)
Screenplay by
Joseph L. Mankiewicz.
Produced by Darryl F.
Zanuck. Directed by
Joseph L. Mankiewicz.
(20th Century Fox) 138 m.

struggle of a woman fighting to save her love life and her career.

As if art and life didn't imitate one another enough on this film, Davis fell in love with and subsequently married her leading man, Gary Merrill. Less happily, as Margo loses a role to Eve in the film, so Davis missed out on the Best Actress Oscar, because she and Anne Baxter split the vote.

The role of Margo Channing, the Queen of Broadway who is trying to hold onto her throne, in All About Eve, *was written for Claudette Colbert, but Bette Davis, a last-minute replacement, more than made the part her own.*

RAIDERS OF THE LOST ARK

Tom Selleck was the first choice for Indiana Jones, the hero of director Steven Spielberg and producer George Lucas' three-film salute to the cliffhanger serials they loved so much as children. But there were difficulties with the star of TV's *Magnum P.I.*, and Harrison Ford, a young character actor and onetime carpenter, got the role that made him famous.

Part of the appeal of these thrill-packed, exhilarating movies that began with *Raiders of the Lost Ark* (1981) and continued with *Indiana Jones and the Temple of Doom* (1984) and *Indiana Jones and the Last Crusade* (1989) was the way they chuckled at the outrageousness of serial plots and B-movie sets. This was where Ford fit in. He was as robust and assured as the actors who played the larger-than-life roles after which Indiana is patterned. But there was a hint of boyish nervousness in his interpretation of the archaeologist-cum-adventurer that was enormously appealing and lifesize (it was also apparent in other films, such as the 1986 *Witness*). It gave the role a casual air that, like a subtle wink, reminded the audience that "It's all in fun." This sort of tongue-in-cheek attitude is what makes Indiana's fear of snakes so funny and believable and what makes so uproarious the moment in the first film when Indiana point-blank shoots a fancy swordsman dead. Indy's lighter side could probably have emerged with Selleck as well, but he could never have managed the undercurrent of gravity that Ford brings to all his roles. That quality gave the Indiana Jones movies their emotional thrust. In short, creating Indiana Jones looked easy. But, like all good tricks, it was a complex, exhilarating feat that Harrison Ford pulled off with flying colors and sustained through two sequels.

Raiders of the Lost Ark
(1981)
Screenplay by Lawrence Kasdan, based on a story by George Lucas and Phillip Kaufman. Produced by Frank Marshall. Directed by Steven Spielberg.
(Paramount) 115 m.

As Indiana Jones in three movies, Harrison Ford harked back to the robust, self-assured idols of the 1930s cliffhangers, with his own hint of boyish nervousness thrown in. Here he protects his sweetheart (Karen Allen) in the film that began the trilogy, Raiders of the Lost Ark.

DRACULA

The great silent star Lon Chaney was set to play Bram Stoker's Dracula, Transylvanian nobleman and bloodthirsty vampire. When Chaney died, he was replaced by an almost unknown Hungarian actor named Bela Lugosi, who had played the role on stage. Whether the extraordinary chance that befell the actor was fortunate or unfortunate is debatable. To be sure it brought him fame and money, but he was so completely right for the role that he would never have much success playing anything else. Thus, as Dracula was destined to live forever sucking the blood of others, Lugosi was fated to play the count, or variations on him, throughout his career. If ever an actor were trapped in a role, it was he.

Part of the reason might be that Lugosi's screen presence was quite narrow in scope. He was a slow, lugubrious actor, whose movement and speech had the perfect hypnotic rhythm for Dracula (the speech pattern was partly dictated by his initially poor command of English). And his darkly handsome face, complete with sleek black hair that formed a widow's peak, suggested a perverse mixture of sexuality and deadly menace. Given his limitations as an actor, he was perfect for a vampire, but unsuited to greater subtleties. Lugosi was soon reduced to playing crude knockoffs of the count in grade-Z films. He ended his career as a drug addict, starring in the offerings of perhaps the world's worst director, Edward D. Wood. He was buried in his cape.

If moviegoers refused to accept Bela Lugosi as anyone but the count, he achieved film immortality in the role. Few who have seen him in it can forget the intensity of his gaze as he eyes inviting necks or the mellifluous tones of his voice as he urges his guests to "Listen to the children of the night. Are they not beautiful?"

Dracula
(1931)
Scenario by Garrett Fort, from the novel by Bram Stoker and the play by Hamilton Deane and John Balderston. Directed by Tod Browning (Universal) 84 m.

Bela Lugosi was an almost unknown Hungarian actor when he played the King of the Undead in Dracula. *He became so closely associated with the role due, in part, to his own limitations as an actor that he was rarely allowed to play anything but the vampire—or variations of him—until his death 25 years after the film's premiere.*

By the time they made *Adam's Rib* together, Spencer Tracy and Katharine Hepburn had been well-established for years as a romantic team on-screen, as well as a secretly happy couple in real life. This mixture of public and private intimacy, coupled with a close, almost conspiratorial working relationship with their director, George Cukor (one of Hepburn's closest friends) and their writers, Garson Kanin and Ruth Gordon (themselves married), made *Adam's Rib* something of a very good club project.

As Adam and Amanda Bonner, married lawyers on opposite sides of an attempted manslaughter case, Tracy and Hepburn were entirely at ease with one another. Their physical familiarity, as in the scene where Adam whacks Amanda on the rear end during a rubdown, was startlingly frank for its time (and remains so today), and their overlapping verbal byplay was—and is—exhilarating. Part of their ability to step so smoothly into their roles

The screen's most legendary couple, Spencer Tracy and Katharine Hepburn, played married lawyers on opposite sides of an attempted murder case in the Kanin–Gordon comedy Adam's Rib.

Tracy and Hepburn made their last screen appearance together in the 1967 comedy about racial prejudice, Guess Who's Coming to Dinner. *Tracy died shortly after filming was completed.*

>>>>>>>>>>>

Adam's Rib
(1949)
Screenplay by Garson Kanin and Ruth Gordon. Produced by Lawrence Weingarten. Directed by George Cukor.
(MGM) 101 m.

must be attributed to Kanin and Gordon, who shrewdly molded their characters to fit the personalities of the stars. Like the staunch political conservative that Tracy was, Adam is the upholder of trusted values and respect for the law. And like the New England liberal that Hepburn was brought up to be, Amanda carries the torch for equal rights and the spirit of change.

This easy blending of reel and real was the basis for one of the frankest and most hilarious portraits of marriage ever put on film.

Tracy and Hepburn were so intimate with one another on-screen that they seemed to hardly be acting at all. Here they are pictured in the first of their collaborations, he as a sportswriter and she as a career woman in Woman of the Year *(1942).*

❧ BEN-HUR ❧

Over the years, Charlton Heston's declamatory line readings, as well as his association with numerous biblical films, have made him the object of quite a few jokes. But it is hard to think of another actor who projected a similar sense of towering strength and fortitude the way Heston did in such out-sized roles as Andrew Jackson in *The President's Lady* (1953) and Moses in *The Ten Commandments* (1956). Indeed, Heston is a heroic, larger-than-life actor if ever there was one, and in no role was he more effective than that of the benign, sober Judah Ben-Hur, a Jewish nobleman of Nazareth who is wrongly imprisoned by his childhood Roman friend Messala (Stephen Boyd). Heston's Judah was truly monumental and he won an Oscar for his work.

The hero of the Lew Wallace novel is an innately wise man who was a contemporary of Jesus; his goodness was constant, even during the torture of prison and slavery. He finally gets his revenge during the chariot race with Messala, which became one of the most famous and exciting scenes in

Charlton Heston trained with stuntmen for weeks to prepare for the climactic chariot race in Ben-Hur, *one of the most exciting sequences ever put on film. Here he wards off the stinging blows from the whip of his friend-turned-bitter enemy Messala (Stephen Boyd).*

movie history. To prepare for this climactic event, Heston trained with stuntmen for weeks and his preparation served him well. The actual filming of the race was enor-mously difficult, and resulted in some real, near-fatal injuries.

But Heston's performance was distinguished by more than an ability to meet the role's physical challenges. He con-

38

vincingly han-dled Judah's transformation from content-ment and hap-piness to pride-ful vengeance. And if he lacks subtlety as an actor, he com-pensates by making believ-able, lines of dialogue that would sound ridiculous in the mouths of others. Perhaps more than any other actor, Heston works on a grand scale. In mo-ments like the one in which

Judah is lauded by the emperor of Rome for saving the life of naval captain Quintus Arrius (Jack Hawkins), it is no disservice to the actor to say that he suggests a statue come to life.

ABOVE: *Heston projected his customary towering strength as Michelangelo in the 1965 adaptation of* The Agony and the Ecstasy.

Ben-Hur
(1959)
Screenplay by Karl Tunberg, based on the novel by Lew Wallace. Produced by Sam Zimbalist. Directed by William Wyler.
(MGM) 217 m.

Heston is a heroic, larger-than-life actor if ever there was one, and in no film was that more evident than in Cecil B. DeMille's The Ten Commandments *(1956), in which he played Moses delivering the He-brews from the land of bondage.*

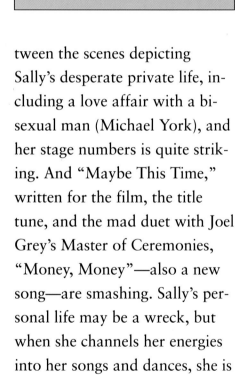

Cabaret
(1972)
Screenplay by Jay Presson Allen, based on the Broadway musical and the book *Goodbye to Berlin* by Christopher Isherwood and the play *I Am a Camera* by John van Druten. Music by John Kander, lyrics by Fred Ebb. Produced by Cy Feuer. Directed by Bob Fosse.
(Allied Artists) 123 m.

When the Broadway musical *Cabaret* was being cast, Liza Minnelli was considered for the role of Sally Bowles, cabaret entertainer and aspiring film star in decadent pre-Nazi Berlin, but in the original show the character was British, so Jill Haworth assayed the part. However, for the film, the show's creators, John Kander and Fred Ebb, reconceived Sally to suit their favorite star. It was a wise decision: Minnelli brought a gushing emotionalism to her performance, as well as an all-stops-out showmanship that the character lacked on the stage. As a consequence, she won a well-deserved Oscar.

Minnelli based her look for the film on cinema stars of the 1920s, such as Louise Brooks and Lya di Putti, and she certainly looked appropriate for the period in this acerbic, ultimately devastating musical. But her connection to the mixed-up, thrill-seeking Sally seemed more than just physical. She brought to the role the same trembling emotionalism that her mother, Judy Garland, had lent to all of her film appearances, and then some. Indeed, Minnelli seemed at times on the verge of nervous collapse in this movie. The contrast between the scenes depicting Sally's desperate private life, including a love affair with a bisexual man (Michael York), and her stage numbers is quite striking. And "Maybe This Time," written for the film, the title tune, and the mad duet with Joel Grey's Master of Ceremonies, "Money, Money"—also a new song—are smashing. Sally's personal life may be a wreck, but when she channels her energies into her songs and dances, she is electrifying.

Minnelli, who got her first big break with Kander and Ebb's stage show, *Flora the Red Menace,* and has starred on Broadway in several of the team's subsequent musicals, has never equalled on-screen her performance in *Cabaret,* perhaps because the role fit her so perfectly.

Liza Minnelli won an Oscar for her dynamic performance as the eccentric Sally Bowles, an American nightclub singer in Weimar Germany in Cabaret.

Jean Harlow represented a particular type of 1930s brassiness better than any other actress. Her characters were brazen and inelegant: when they paraded their finery, there was never a doubt where it came from—men. In her few dramatic appearances, films like *Hell's Angels* (1930) and *The Public Enemy* (1931), she did not make much of an impression. Rather, she came alive in comedies, where her frank sexuality and gold-digging ways were allowed to flourish without censorial punishment.

Kitty Packard in *Dinner at Eight* was perhaps the quintessence of the Harlow woman. She is the kept wife of the gruff Dan Packard (Wallace Beery), forever lounging in expensive negligees and pyjamas in an impossibly elegant bedroom. She and her roughhouse husband trade gutter-mouthed insults ("You big windbag!" she screams) while she feigns sick-

Dinner at Eight
(1933)
Screenplay by Frances Marion and Herman J. Mankiewicz, based on the play by George S. Kaufman and Edna Ferber. Directed by George Cukor.
(MGM) 113 m.

of her husband), Harlow's Kitty was the epitome of raucous sexuality. In the film's final moments, as Kitty walks to dinner

Jean Harlow was hilarious as Kitty Packard, a golddigger holding court in her well-earned boudoir in Dinner at Eight.

ness, hoping for a visit from Dr. Talbot (Edmund Lowe), with whom she is having an affair. With her platinum blonde hair, doll-like face, perfect figure, and hilariously tinny voice (dropping to a childish pout whenever she wants to wheedle something out

with the matronly Carlotta Vance (Marie Dressler), she tells her of a book she's been reading about how machines may someday take over every job in the world. "Oh, my dear," says Carlotta, "that's something you need never worry about."

Jack Lemmon's C.C. Baxter was an everyman for the late 1950s, a straight-arrow organization man MacLaine) is one of those who comes to his place for trysts. Lemmon's buoyantly nervous touch gave the film and the character a pathos that is barely imaginable with any other actor. He did a wonderful job of suggesting Baxter's surprise in the end, when he discovers what the audience already knew—that he is actually a decent guy at heart.

Lemmon had worked with acerbic director Billy Wilder the year before in *Some Like It Hot*, and the part in *The Apartment* was written for him. He had already demonstrated

ABOVE: *Shortly after breaking into films, Lemmon won a Best Supporting Actor Oscar, playing Ensign Pulver, the ship's madcap laundry and morale officer in* Mister Roberts *(1955). Here he gleefully tells Doc (William Powell, left) and Doug Roberts (Henry Fonda, right) about the results of his latest hair-brained scheme.*

who wants to preserve the status quo and rise smoothly up the corporate ladder. When opportunity knocks, this lowly clerk in a large company is even willing to rise through the ranks by lending his apartment to his superiors for extramarital romps—only to find that the object of his affection (Shirley

RIGHT: *Jack Lemmon's C. C. Baxter was an everyman for the late 1950s, a straight-arrow organization man who wants to rise smoothly up the corporate ladder. All that is standing in his way is his own innate decency, which he discovers when he falls in his love with elevator operator Fran Kubelik (Shirley MacLaine).*

⫸⫸⫸⫸⫸⫸⫸⫸

The Apartment
(1960)
Screenplay by Billy Wilder
and I. A. L. Diamond.
Produced and directed by
Billy Wilder.
(United Artists) 125 m.

his talents in similar roles, most notably his Oscar-winning performance in *Mister Roberts* (1955). But *The Apartment* was a workout—Lemmon would describe the emotionally com-

During the 1950s Jack Lemmon was primarily known as a comic actor, but he convincingly showed his ability to handle drama when he played a down-and-out alcoholic in Days of Wine and Roses *(1962).*

plex, frenzied scene in which Baxter tries to revive MacLaine's Fran Kubelik after she has attempted suicide with sleeping pills as the most demanding of his career. For example, the film was blessed with inspired on-the-set invention (despite Wilder's strict adherence to his written words).

The running gin game be-

tween Baxter and Kubelik, which ends the film—the audience never sees the characters kiss—was incorporated into the script because Lemmon and MacLaine were always playing cards on the set.

ANNIE HALL

Contrary to popular belief, Woody Allen and Diane Keaton were not in love during or just previous to the filming of *Annie Hall*. They had, however, dated each other several years earlier. Perhaps it was the intimacy of their friendship that enabled them to create one of the most cherished love stories of the last 20 years.

Annie Hall
(1977)
Screenplay by Woody Allen and Marshall Brickman. Produced by Fred T. Callo. Directed by Woody Allen. (United Artists) 93 m.

Alvy and Annie are an odd couple who meet during an indoor tennis game. He is a New York Jew, she a Wisconsin WASP; she embraces popular culture, which he disdains. What they do share are neuroses and a lack of confidence, and these become the bases for their love affair.

The mixture of romantic longing and nebbishy self-doubt in *Annie Hall* not only made this comedy a milestone for a generation of people, it marked the maturation of Allen as both a director and an actor. Alvy was the first character that he conceived for himself who was not completely jokey. He is funny, to be sure, but he is also a recognizable and attractive human being with human foibles (his childhood fear that the universe is expanding, his obsession with death). And Allen the director used many film

techniques—subtitles (to convey what's going on in Alvy's and Annie's heads as they talk), characters meeting people from their past, animation—to further his charming essay on romance.

Alvy and Annie fumbling with lobsters during a stay in Cape Cod (Allen and Keaton were genuinely terrified) or bickering on line to see *The Sorrow and the Pity* are now classic moments in romantic cinema. Aside from the film's many quotable lines, most of them coming from Alvy ("Don't knock masturbation—it's sex with someone I love," being perhaps the most memorable) or Annie's taste in bargain-basement clothes, which inspired an instant and inexpensive fashion trend, Allen and Keaton created a naturalistic, fluid portrait of bittersweet romance that seems to surpass acting.

Woody Allen as Alvy Singer and Diane Keaton as Annie Hall are sweetly tentative lovers in the now classic film, Annie Hall.

M

In America Peter Lorre was known as a thin, ethereal character actor of indeterminate European origin, usually a small, insinuating companion to the rotund Sydney Greenstreet. In *The Maltese Falcon* (1941), for example, they made a macabre pair of international crooks, operating on the same exotic, diabolical wave-length. Lorre's famous bug eyes, childish grin, doll-like face, and otherworldly voice made him a fringe presence of great renown in Hollywood films, but his character always seemed to be hovering somewhere around the periphery of the action, never at its center.

That was not so, however, in the German film *M*. Lorre played a baby-faced child murderer (based on the real-life Peter Kurten) who is stalked by both the police and the criminal population of Berlin. This psy-

from limb, he screams, "Who knows what it feels like to be me? How I'm forced to act . . ."

Although Lorre paid a price for his compelling portrayal by being typecast in similar

Peter Lorre is Hans Beckert, a child murderer facing possible punishment by an ad-hoc tribunal of Berlin criminals in Fritz Lang's M.

M
(1931)
Scenario and dialogue by Thea Von Harbou, after an article by Egon Jacobson. Produced by Nero Film A. G. Directed by Fritz Lang.
(Nero Film) 99 m.

chopath initially inspires horror in the audience as he walks the streets, kindly offering candy and balloons to unsuspecting children. But by the film's end, as he is hunted down like a wild animal, he inspires compassion. Cowering against a roomfull of bloodthirsty criminals ready to tear him limb

roles throughout his career, few actors in the movies have ever delivered such a compelling portrait of a human being at the mercy of his own impulses. One can almost feel the ecstasy of Lorre's killer as he approaches his victims, like a dope fiend getting ready for his fix.

TO KILL A MOCKINGBIRD

Gregory Peck has come to represent absolute goodness and wisdom on the screen, using his craggy face and deep, soothing baritone to make men of stature believable and admirable. Indeed, his espousal of liberal causes (he was on

> **To Kill a Mockingbird**
> (1962)
> Screenplay by Horton Foote, from a novel by Harper Lee. Produced by Alan J. Pakula. Directed by Robert Mulligan. (Universal) 129 m.

Richard Nixon's famous enemies list) has caused more than one person to suggest that he run for president on the Democratic ticket. So far, at least, he hasn't done that, but he did play the nation's chief executive in the 1987 film *Amazing Grace and Chuck*.

The role that typecast Peck as the worldly philosopher king of the movies was Atticus Finch in *To Kill a Mockingbird*. Finch was based on the real-life Amasa Lee, whose daughter Harper wrote the novel on which the film was based. Peck worked closely with Lee (who based the character of Scout on herself as a young girl and the character of Dill on her childhood friend, Truman Capote).

Atticus is a single father and lawyer in the South in the

Gregory Peck won an Oscar for his portrayal of Atticus Finch, the morally unimpeachable southern lawyer in To Kill a Mockingbird, *based on the novel by Harper Lee.*

Four years after Peck's long film career began, he played a reporter writing an exposé on anti-Semitism in Gentleman's Agreement *(1947). It brought him his third Oscar nomination. He is pictured here with actress Anne Revere, who played his mother.*

1920s who defends a black man named Tom Robinson (Brock Peters), against the charges of raping a local white girl. As Atticus tries his case in court, he also combats the fury of the local white community, which thinks his client should simply be strung up. Peck played the role with a stern, gentle authority, characterized by more than one critic as Lincolnesque (indeed, the scene in which Atticus wards off a lynch mob as he calmly sits on the jailhouse porch is very close to a scene in 1939's *Young Mr. Lincoln*).

Lee was delighted with the film and with Peck, who won an Oscar for his performance. But from time to time the actor has appeared disappointed that no one seems to remember him in his bad-guy roles, such as Lute in *Duel in the Sun* (1946) and Richard Wilson in *The Macomber Affair* (1947). He will just have to reconcile himself, it seems, to the fact that he will forever be linked to good, decent men like Atticus Finch in the minds of his fans.

Peck underwent a radical change of pace for the challenging role of the indomitable Captain Ahab in director John Huston's adaptation of Herman Melville's Moby Dick *(1956).*

Humphrey Bogart was a contract player who worked long and hard at Warner Brothers throughout the 1930s before he got his

Bogart solidified his stardom in 1941 with a role that had been turned down by George Raft, that of Roy Earle, the aging bank robber, in High Sierra *(1941).*

break in 1941 in director John Huston's debut film. The actor may have first gained public attention with *The Petrified Forest* (1936) but it was in *The Maltese Falcon* that the Bogart mystique was born. Ironically, the part was initially offered to George Raft, who turned it down because he didn't want to work with a novice director.

Another of Raft's leavings, *High Sierra*, also released in 1941, helped Bogart solidify his new stardom.

Tough, cynical, smart, unsentimental—these attributes describe Sam Spade, the San Francisco private eye who gets mixed up with a bunch of ruthless international treasure hunters, but they came to define the Bogart persona as well. Audiences found him different from Cagney and Robinson, the other reigning tough guys of the movies. He was less ingratiating, more thoughtful. His characters were usually loners, prone to introspection, and disdainful of sentimentality. Certainly no one could have accused Spade, one of the most cynical roles Bogart ever played, of being a warmhearted guy. His partner's body isn't even cold yet before the man's name is being taken off the door. And, al-

The Maltese Falcon
(1941)
Screenplay by John Huston, based on the novel by Dashiell Hammett. Executive Producer, Hal B. Wallis. Associate Producer, Henry Blanke. Directed by John Huston.
(Warner Bros.) 100 m.

though Sam falls in love with the most treacherous of all his clients, the lying Brigid O'Shaughnessy (Mary Astor), he is not above sending her up the river for murder in the end. Still, when he bids goodbye to her, saying he'll be sad "if they hang that pretty little neck of yours," Bogart's face and voice endow the moment with a tragic quality that no other actor of the day could have provided. From Cagney, for example, the farewell would have been a gleeful taunt.

Humphrey Bogart and Katharine Hepburn are pictured here in The African Queen *(1951). Bogart won his first and only Oscar as the irascible ship's captain, Charlie Allnut.*

Humphrey Bogart became a major star after appearing as Sam Spade, the cynical detective in the adaptation of Dashiell Hammett's The Maltese Falcon.

In the final analysis, it was that extra dimension that Bogart provided, the romantic beneath the cynic, the man who expects nothing from his fellow human beings but winds up disappointed nonetheless, that distinguished him throughout his long career.

Bogart got his first big break in The Petrified Forest *(1936), in which he re-created his Broadway role as the murderous Duke Mantee. Leslie Howard,* center, *helped him get the part. Bette Davis is at left.*

In the mid-1960s, Julie Andrews became Hollywood's symbol of sweetness and light, the embodiment of virginal purity with a crystal clear soprano voice and apple-cheeked freshness. She might have remained famous for the role she didn't get—Eliza Doolittle in the film version of *My Fair Lady,* which she had created on Broadway— had she not been given two plum film roles that would forever

ing out on Eliza; and, of course, Maria in *The Sound of Music.*

The opening scene of the movie, in which Maria ambles across a green alpine mountaintop singing the first bars of the title song, has become so familiar over the years that it was parodied in the opening animation of *The Return of*

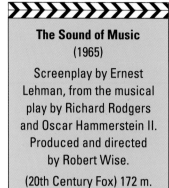

The Sound of Music
(1965)
Screenplay by Ernest Lehman, from the musical play by Richard Rodgers and Oscar Hammerstein II. Produced and directed by Robert Wise.
(20th Century Fox) 172 m.

years, she was enchanting and effective in the role of the governess who wins the hearts of the Von Trapp children and eventually the hand of their stern father (Christopher Plummer) in 1938 Austria. Andrews' embodiment of unimpeachable goodness in the film is embedded in the memories of a generation that flocked to see it as children, as are her renditions of some of the infectious Rodgers and Hammerstein songs, particularly "Do-Re-Mi" and "My Favorite Things."

LEFT: *Andrews won a compensatory Oscar for her portrayal of the magical governess in Walt Disney's* Mary Poppins *(1964) after she lost the role of Eliza Doolittle in the film version of her Broadway hit,* My Fair Lady, *to Audrey Hepburn.*

OPPOSITE: *As Maria in* The Sound of Music, *Julie Andrews became the embodiment of unimpeachable goodness for a generation that flocked to see the film as youngsters. Here the understanding governess comforts the youngest of the Von Trapp children who is having difficulty sleeping.*

color her movie image: *Mary Poppins* (1964), the Disney musical for which she won an Oscar as a sort of compensation for losing the Pink Panther (1975), directed by Andrews' husband, Blake Edwards. But for all the fun that has been poked at Andrews over the

⇜ SMOKEY AND THE BANDIT ⇝

Burt Reynolds had a long yet tentative career in television, which included a stint as the blacksmith on *Gunsmoke*, before he hit his stride on the big screen in the l970s. It was his solid performance in *Deliverance* in 1972 that finally established him as something more than a Marlon

ways displayed a flair, even on the talk show circuit, where he has occasionally served as a guest host. The peak of his popularity came in 1977 with the broad good-ole-boy movie *Smokey and the Bandit*. Indeed, it made him one of the biggest stars in movies.

Smokey and the Bandit is

>>>>>>>>>>>>>>>>>>>>>>>>>

Smokey and the Bandit

(1977)

Screenplay by James Lee Barrett, Charles Shyer, and Alan Mandel. Produced by Robert L. Levy. Directed by Hal Needham. (Universal) 97 m.

In 1977, Burt Reynolds reached the peak of his popularity as a movie star with the broad good-ole-boy comedy Smokey and the Bandit, *in which he played an easygoing bootlegger being pursued by a hot-tempered sheriff (Jackie Gleason).*

Brando look-alike. Thereafter, he did well in action pictures, but he was particularly adept at comedy, for which he has al-

basically a long car chase directed by a former second-unit stunt specialist, Hal Needham. Jackie Gleason is the "Smokey"—CB

slang for a highway patrolman—an easily exasperated southern sheriff who is in hot, prolonged pursuit of the Bandit (Burt Reynolds), a bootlegger who has run off with his son's fiancée (Sally Field). Gleason's short-fuse routine worked well against Reynolds' effortlessly charming smart aleck—the Bandit is a sort of Wile E. Coyote to the Smokey's Roadrunner. Sporting a boyish grin and a Clark Gable moustache, Reynolds was at his most winning when he delivered his incongruously high-pitched, open-mouthed laugh. There were two sequels, only one more with Reynolds. After that he and director Needham were busy with *Smokey*-inspired concoctions like *The Cannonball Run* (1981), leaving Gleason to play both Smokey *and* the Bandit in the concluding episode.

Director Billy Wilder's original choice for the role of Norma Desmond was Mae West, who was insulted that she should be asked to play the role of someone no longer in her prime. He also sought out Pola Negri and Mary Pickford, but it was Gloria

Sunset Boulevard
(1950)
Screenplay by Charles Brackett, Billy Wilder, and D. M. Marshman, Jr. Produced by Charles Brackett. Directed by Billy Wilder.
(Paramount) 110 m.

Swanson who jumped at the chance to portray the faded star of Hollywood's bygone days who madly clings to her stardom in a life of tawdry splendor. As Norma awaits that next big part which will never come, she meets a down-at-the-heels, acerbic screenwriter named Joe Gillis and engages him to write her grandiose comeback. Wilder wanted Montgomery Clift to play Gillis, who narrates the

flashback action as a corpse floating in a swimming pool, but Clift dropped out before shooting started. Gene Kelly also refused the part, and it went to William Holden.

The contrast in acting styles—Swanson's florid, gesticulating hamminess and Holden's prosaic naturalism—helped emphasize the differences between the two protagonists. Where Swanson's characteristic gesture as Norma was a grandly emphatic sweep of her arm, Holden's for Joe was a shrug with arms folded. Where Norma's voice expands with rhetorical fervor, Joe's remains in that cynical, sandpapery deadpan that was one of Holden's trademarks throughout his career. It was

the very incompatibility that Swanson and Holden projected so forcefully that made them one of the screen's most enduring, if improbable, couples.

The haunting Sunset Boulevard *featured one of the screen's most enduring, if improbable, couples—Gloria Swanson as aging star Norma Desmond and William Holden as the young screenwriter, Joe Gillis. The contrast between the stars' methods of acting helped accentuate the gulf between their characters.*

Whalen director William Wellman started his 1930 gangster movie *Beer and Blood*, he cast Edward Woods in the lead and James Cagney, a young Warner Brothers' contract player, as his sidekick. After just one day of shooting, Wellman and his writers convinced production chief Darryl F. Zanuck that the actors should switch parts.

Beer and Blood became *The Public Enemy*, it was released to widespread acclaim, and Cagney became a phenomenon almost instantly. The reason for his instant success is

Throughout his career, Cagney thought of himself first and foremost as a song and dance man. He showed why, in his own inimitable style, playing George M. Cohan in the 1942 musical Yankee Doodle Dandy, *which earned him an Oscar.*

not hard to understand. As Tom Powers (he based his portrayal on Chicago mobster Dion O'Bannion), Cagney came on like a force of nature, so apparently effortless was his talent, so physical was his acting. True, his persona was in

Cagney had become a major star at Warner Bros. by the time he appeared in the role of Rocky Sullivan, the kid from the wrong side of the tracks who grows up to be a gangster, in Angels with Dirty Faces *(1938).*

Tom Powers (James Cagney) delivers
that legendary grapefruit to his girlfriend's kisser in The Public Enemy.

raw, budding form in this, his fifth film, and his line readings were not quite as cocksure as they would become just a year later in movies like *Blonde Crazy* or *Taxi!*, but the natural grace and the mixture of charm and treachery were already fully developed. So was the spontaneity that would characterize his acting through 40 years on screen. A prime exam-

ple is the famous moment in which Tom plants a grapefruit in his girl's face. It is performed in one deft, unhesitating motion delivered right to the kisser and pushed in with panache to spare. The scene, which became something of a trademark for

the actor, was apparently cooked up as a gag for the crew by Cagney and the "girlfriend," Mae Clarke, and shot in one take. For the rest of his life, Cagney received complimentary grapefruits whenever he went to restaurants.

>>>>>>>>>>>>

The Public Enemy
(1931)
Story by Kubec Glasmon and John Bright. Adaptation by Harvey Thew. Directed by William Wellman.
(Warner Bros.) 84 m.

- - - -

At the heart of *The Silence of the Lambs* are the exchanges between special FBI agent Clarice Starling, who is tracking down a serial killer, and Dr. Hannibal Lecter, a brilliant psychiatrist who is himself a deadly serial killer. These conversations take place at the end of a long, dark prison corridor, where Clarice sits outside Lecter's maximum security cell, enduring the pain of being psychologically dissected by "Hannibal the Cannibal" in exchange for a few of his uniquely brilliant insights into the mind of a homicidal sociopath.

Working from stillness, British actor Anthony Hopkins

Clarice Starling (Jodie Foster), an FBI agent pursuing a serial killer, endures the probes and taunts of a brilliant but deranged psychiatrist in order to gain insight into her quarry. Foster's ability to convey her character's vulnerability as well as her strength helps make her encounters with Hopkins' psychiatrist absolutely riveting.

OF THE LAMBS

The Silence of the Lambs
(1991)
Screenplay by Ted Tally,
based on the novel by
Thomas Harris. Produced
by Kenneth Utt,
Edward Saxon, and Ron
Bozman. Directed by
Jonathan Demme.
(Orion) 118 m.

played Lecter as an evil genius whose intellect is at the service of his carnivorous appetites. With his hair slicked back and his mouth perpetually open in a chilling half-grin, he questions Clarice in an ominously lighter-than-air voice (which Hopkins based on that of Katharine Hepburn), then closes his eyes and sighs with orgasmic delight as she delivers up another personal detail.

Jodie Foster's Clarice, poised, professional, and courteous, registers the effect of every probe and painful insight with the sensitivity of a seismograph. Wending her way through a thicket of challenging encounters, the actress maintains a difficult balance between delicacy and toughness, pragmatism and vengeful passion, at once the hardened skeptic and the wide-eyed rube. The result gives Hop-

Anthony Hopkins
played Dr. Hannibal Lecter, the psychiatrist turned serial
killer. With his hair slicked back and his mouth perpetually open in a
chilling half-grin, the skilled British actor stripped away the defenses
of Foster's young FBI agent using an ominously lighter-than-air voice
based on that of Katharine Hepburn.

kins an opponent more than capable of matching him in games of intricate, psychological hide-and-seek that become so intimate, they seem eerily like love scenes.

Hopkins and Foster received Oscars for their performances. It was the sixth time in Academy Award history that both leads in a film were so honored.

GILDA

Rita Hayworth was the apple of Columbia boss Harry Cohn's eye in the mid-1940s when she played the alluring title character in *Gilda*. Consequently, she got the sort of glamour treatment that had previously been reserved for European imports like Garbo and Dietrich. The result certainly showed. As Gilda, Hayworth looked utterly bewitching in every frame of every scene in which she appeared.

Although the film was written page by page, the actors never knowing their dialogue until the day of shooting, there was nothing sloppy about the finished product. Gilda is, as they used to say, a "tramp" who has jilted Johnny Farrell (Glenn Ford) in America only to find him again in Buenos Aires, where he is working for Mundson (George Macready), the mad casino owner that Gilda has married for money. Gilda and Johnny torture one another with cruelty and teasing, constantly proclaiming their hatred, while beneath the surface their mutual passion swirls. Director Charles Vidor told his actors to think dirty thoughts during their scenes, and that bit of inspired coaching helped. Hayworth smiled through all of Gilda's sexual taunts to Johnny, making her that much more infuriating— and desirable. She brought to the role (in addition to her beautiful face and a sumptuous body clad in tight-fitting gowns throughout) a sense of confidence and a burning desire to bust loose. Her supreme moment, in the scene that defined her as a screen personality, was the musical number "Put the Blame on Mame," a prelude to a striptease. It is a public provocation aimed at Johnny, who has married her and scorned her. As Hayworth played it, it was a personal declaration of independence.

Gilda
(1946)
Screenplay by Marion Parsonnet. Produced by Virginia Van Upp. Directed by Charles Vidor.
(Columbia) 110 m.

In her most famous moment on film, Rita Hayworth puts "The Blame on Mame" as she begins the climactic striptease in Gilda.

S hocking as it may seem now, *The Adventures of Robin Hood* was originally planned and designed for James Cagney, who was Warner Brothers' biggest star in the late 1930s. But Cagney was engaged in a contract war with the studio bosses and refused to do the picture. He would certainly have made a funny, flamboyant, and athletic Robin. But could he ever have mustered the heroic stature, the storybook charm, or, with all due respect, the English manner that have made Errol Flynn virtually synonymous with the role?

The Australian actor's star was on the rise after *Captain Blood* (1935), and he fit the similarly swashbuckling role of the legendary Robin to perfection. With his natural charm, dashing good looks, and wonderful smile, Flynn made one believe that his nobleman-turned-outlaw could indeed take on the world. During the sequence in which he battles the evil Prince John (Claude Rains) and his cousin Sir Guy, the Sheriff of Nottingham (Basil Rathbone) first with wordplay, then with swordplay, his lusty good cheer is utterly infectious.

All attempts by others to play the part in a more realistic fashion (most notably Kevin Costner, who strikes a downbeat, dourly modern note in the 1991 *Robin Hood: Prince of Thieves*) just make Flynn's agile, outsized Robin shine that much more brightly.

> **The Adventures of Robin Hood**
> (1938)
> Screenplay by Norman Reilly Raine and Seton I. Miller, based on the Robin Hood legends. Produced by Hal B. Wallis and Henry Blanke. Directed by Michael Curtiz and William Keighley.
> (Warner Bros.) 102 m.

Robin Hood (Errol Flynn, left) engages in mortal combat with the evil Sir Guy (Basil Rathbone) to climax the spirited The Adventures of Robin Hood. *Flynn's dashing, good-humored nobleman-turned-outlaw established the benchmark against which all other Robins have been measured.*

Saturday Night Fever
(1977)
Screenplay by Norman Wexler, based on a story by Nick Cohn. Produced by Milt Felsen. Directed by John Badham.
(Paramount) 119 m.

Now that disco music is long dead, *Saturday Night Fever* has become a period piece. But at the time of its release in 1977, one either absolutely loved it or absolutely hated it, depending on one's feelings about the style of music that it helped to foster. And the same went for its star, who must have been doing something right to inspire such passion.

In a sense, Travolta's situation at the time mirrored Tony Manero's, the character he played. Manero is a Brooklyn hardware store employee trying to break out of the local disco scene to make it as a dancer on Broadway, while Travolta was trying to break out of television and make it in films. And Travolta was every bit as flamboyant a screen personality as the character

Manero. The actor's cocky walk and often-mimicked loose vocal inflections seemed Brooklyn homegrown, although Travolta is actually from New Jersey, and there was a real pathos in his portrayal of a young man who is learning the hard way that the world is not quite going to meet his expectations (at the time, the actor had just lost his lover, actress Diana Hyland, to cancer).

But it was on the dance floor that Travolta,

like his character, truly reigned. A sleek and graceful dancer, he trained rigorously for the role, having never done any disco dancing before. It is small wonder that the actor was James Cagney's choice to play him in a screen biography, should the occasion ever arise.

Travolta reprised Tony Manero in the 1983 sequel *Stayin' Alive*. His luck in other films has been intermittent. For many, he will always be clad in a white leisure suit and platform shoes, his arm pointed in the air and his body angled, bathed in the red glow of the 2001 Disco.

Playing Tony Manero in Saturday Night Fever *made TV actor John Travolta one of the hottest movie stars in the world. This shot of him setting the dance floor on fire became one of the iconic film images of the 1970s.*

All the hoopla over *The Jazz Singer* as the first talking picture tends to obscure the incredible charisma and emotional wallop of Al Jolson's performance in the film. Jolson was an enormously popular vaudeville star who made his debut in the 1923 D. W. Griffith silent, *Mammy Boy*. But his voice was his main draw.

By 1927, the brothers Warner had sunk all of their money into making talking pictures. When they chose Samson Raphaelson's Broadway hit, *The Jazz Singer*, for their maiden effort—featuring only some scenes with sound—they initially tried to enlist George Jessel who had originated the role on the stage. Next they turned to Eddie Cantor, who also turned them down. Finally Jolson took the part and took Warner Brothers to the bank with the result.

Jolson begins the film as Jakie Rabinowitz, the son of an old-world Jewish cantor, played by Warner Oland (soon to be cast as Charlie Chan). Although he is training to follow in his father's footsteps, Jakie is drawn to mod-

Al Jolson broke the sound barrier as Jakie Rabinowitz, the cantor's son who becomes show business star Jack Robin, in the 1927 milestone film, The Jazz Singer.

ern secular music. After changing his name to Jack Robin he leaves home to seek a career as a singer, and his father disowns him.

The film and the role speak eloquently of the cultural frustration felt by many children of European immigrants, drawn as they were to the opportunities of the new world but still tied to the traditions of the old. Jolson's soulful, physical performance beautifully underscores the

theme—his eyes seem to be on fire with a passion for music as well as a love for his mother (May McAvoy). All of Jolson's musical numbers, including "Toot Toot Tootsie" and "Mammy," are showstoppers. Perhaps the film's key moment comes, however, when Jakie returns home to see his mother while his father is out and playfully sings "Blue Skies" to her at the piano. Jolson and McAvoy improvised the scene, which is so spontaneous and fresh that one might be watching a real mother and son.

The story was refilmed twice, once in 1953 with Danny Thomas and again in 1980 with Neil Diamond. The original is still the best by far.

> **The Jazz Singer**
> **(1927)**
> Adaptation by Alfred A. Cohn, titles by Jack Jarmuth, based on the play by Samson Raphaelson. Songs by Irving Berlin, Sam Lewis, Joe Young, Walter Donaldson, Gus Kahn, Ernie Erdman, Dan Russo, Edgar Leslie, Grant Clarke, Al Jolson, Jimmy Monaco, and Louis Silvers. Directed by Alan Crosland.
> (Warner Bros.) 89 m.

Judy Garland was one of MGM's biggest young stars in 1939 when *The Wizard of Oz* was being made, but she was not the first choice for Dorothy, the girl who wants to get back to Kansas after a tornado carries her to the fantastical land of Oz. The studio brass wanted to borrow Shirley Temple from 20th Century Fox for the role, but producer Mervyn LeRoy insisted on and got Garland. At this point in her young career she had already developed a substance abuse problem, thanks to a regimen of diet pills prescribed for her by the studio to control a weight problem. It was Garland's tragic, neurotic edge that gave this most famous of all children's films its poignancy and power.

Garland gave what many believe to be her finest performance as Vicki Lester, the Hollywood singer-actress whose star rises as her husband's falls, in the 1954 remake of A Star Is Born.

Much of Garland's work in films and music seemed to be part skill, part determination, and part neurosis. She was never just a simple, pretty ingenue. Her performance in *Wizard* and, particularly her rendition of "Somewhere Over the Rainbow," were heartbreaking in

One of the many fondly remembered musicals that the mature Judy Garland made at MGM was Easter Parade *(1948). She is pictured here with co-star Fred Astaire, in costume, for the charming "A Couple of Swells" number.*

By the time Garland made Meet Me in St. Louis *in 1944, the executives at MGM had allowed her to become a young woman on-screen. As seen here with young Margaret O'Brien, she never looked lovelier than she did in this turn-of-the-century musical directed by her future husband, Vincente Minnelli.*

their intensity and depth of feeling. And what American who saw the movie on TV once a year as he or she grew up can forget the terror in Dorothy's face as she is in the clutches of Margaret Hamilton's wicked witch, her furious indignation as she exposes Frank Morgan's wizard, or her childlike belief in magic as she taps her ruby slippers together and murmurs, "There's no place like home"? Who can forget the wonderful bonds of kinship she forges with the Tin Man (Jack Haley), the Scarecrow (Ray Bolger), and the Lion (Bert Lahr), or

The Wizard of Oz
(1939)
Screenplay by Florence Ryerson, Noel Langley, and Edgar Allan Wolfe, based on the book by L. Frank Baum. Produced by Mervyn LeRoy. Directed by Victor Fleming.
(MGM) 102 m.

For many, Judy Garland will always be the wistful young girl, clutching her little terrier and trying desperately to find her way back to Kansas in the immortal The Wizard of Oz.

her plaintive sorrow as she sings that emblematic song?

She would go on from this film to have a very successful career as an adult, starring in such memorable movies as *Meet Me in St. Louis* (1944), *Easter Parade* (1948), and *A Star Is Born* (1954), but she is perhaps best remembered as Dorothy Gale, for her performance as the Kansas orphan has come to represent all the happiness, the terror, and the innocence of childhood.

Alfred Hitchcock's original choice for the role of Roger O. Thornhill, the Madison Avenue man who is mistaken for an international spy, was James Stewart. But as the script began to take on increasingly comic overtones (and as Hitchcock's previous film with Stewart, 1958's *Vertigo*, did not do well at the box office), the director turned to his other erstwhile leading man, Cary Grant. Grant had the suave composure needed for the role, as well as the ability to locate its emotional core—a combination of bewilderment, outrage, determination, and unflappability—without exposing it.

The script of *North by Northwest* takes Thornhill from Manhattan to Mount Rushmore via Long Island, a romantic ride on the 20th Century passenger train to Chicago with a mysterious blonde named Eve (Eva Marie Saint), an ambush by a crop duster on a prairie stop en route to Indianapolis, and a phony murder set up to convince his pursuer (James Mason) that he is

As an ad man mistaken for an international spy in Alfred Hitchcock's North by Northwest, *Cary Grant brought just the right mix of bewilderment, outrage, determination, and unflappability to the role. Here he gloats at his pursuers as the Chicago police escort him from a public auction.*

dead. Even Grant expressed be-fuddlement with the turn of events in the script, an attitude that perfectly matched his char-acter's in the movie. This adds considerably to the very special tone of the film, combining as it does genuine suspense, as in the cliffhanger at the climax, and outrageous humor, as in the scene in which the spies get Thornhill drunk and put him behind the wheel of a moving car on a treacherous road.

In every role that Grant played, surface charm and dig-

Grant played his sec-ond role for director Alfred Hitchcock in the 1946 thriller No-torious. *He is an FBI agent who has placed his lover (In-grid Bergman) in mortal peril by hav-ing her infiltrate a group of Nazi agents in Rio de Janeiro.*

nity were givens. In this movie, he used those qualities to make a wild romp out of what might otherwise have seemed harrow-ing. His control was so great that even the slightest inflection could suggest emotion-al depths. In the riveting auction house scene, for instance, the hurt that Thornhill feels over what he sees as Eve's betrayal comes across with an absolute econo-my of expres-sion. Perhaps the film's key image,

and one of Grant's best moments, occurs near the beginning. In the Plaza Hotel, Thornhill and his mother (Jessie Royce Landis, a year younger than Grant at the time) step into an elevator with the two men who are pursuing him. "You're not really trying to kill my son, are you?" asks the mother, at which point everyone in the elevator bursts out laugh-ing except Thornhill. Fear, em-barrassment, and confusion are all expressed by Grant without moving a muscle.

In director Howard Hawks' uproarious screwball comedy Bringing Up Baby *(1938), Grant's charm-ing and dignified comportment as a very proper archaeologist was continually tested by a daffy heiress (Katharine Hepburn), with the two of them chasing a leopard through Connecticut.*

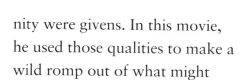
North by Northwest
(1959)
Screenplay by
Ernest Lehman.
Produced and directed
by Alfred Hitchcock.
(MGM) 136 m.

Charles Chaplin came to Hollywood at the behest of Mack Sennett, whose bouncing, frenetic comedies were then gaining popularity. It was in his second Sennett film, *Kid Auto Races at Venice* (1914), that the character of the Little Tramp began to evolve. The short gentleman in tattered clothing and bowler hat, sporting a cane, a seesaw walk, and a tiny moustache, became one of the most recognized figures in the world. He was a symbol of warmth and gentility and the embodiment of a carefree if wistful spirit.

By 1931, when Chaplin filmed *City Lights,* sound had taken hold of the film industry. Only he could have continued to make what is essentially a silent movie (with a few sound effects), so completely were pantomime and physical comedy tied to the success of his character. *City Lights,* which Chaplin would later consider his crowning achievement, was shot on a two-block set that represented an entire city. For many film lovers, it was Chaplin's finest work because it represented his most deft blending of comedy and pathos. In it the Little Tramp meets a beautiful, blind flower girl (Virginia Cherrill, later Mrs. Cary Grant) with whom he falls in

City Lights
(1931)
Conceived, produced, and directed by Charles Chaplin.
(United Artists) 86 m.

In City Lights, *the film that Charles Chaplin himself considered his crowning achievement, the Little Tramp meets a beautiful, blind flower girl (Virginia Cherrill) with whom he falls in love.*

temperamental street elevator, swallowing a whistle and hiccupping in little toots, and stepping into the boxing ring with a big brawler. But the film's most fondly remembered scenes are those of pathos, such as that in which

love and for whom he schemes to get the money she needs for an operation to restore her sight. The raucous, expertly timed physical comedy that became a Chaplin trademark was in full flower here—with the Tramp admiring a statue of a nude in a store window as he stands on a

the Tramp saves the life of a drunken millionaire (Harry Meyers), only to go unrecognized and unacknowledged by the man when he is sober. Most cherished of all, though, is the scene in which the girl sees the Little Tramp's smiling, disheveled, terrified face for the first time.

WALL STREET

Michael Douglas has been good in a number of movies—his errant husband in *Fatal Attraction* (1987) and his heroic cameraman in *The China Syndrome* (1979) come to mind—but his appeal seemed to be somewhat limited to average-guy roles. Quite unlike his intense father, Kirk, one could never imagine Michael playing Vincent van Gogh. His talents seemed better suited to producing, which he has done successfully on several occasions, including *One Flew Over the Cuckoo's Nest* (1975), for which he won an Oscar. Until *Wall Street,* that is. Gordon Gecko in Wall Street represented a remarkable instance of an actor going against type and finding his perfect role. So snugly did Douglas fit the part of the charmingly brazen 1980s corporate raider that the name Gordon Gecko joined the popular vocabulary almost overnight.

Gecko is a shark in gentlemen's clothing, his stylishly long hair slicked back the better to reveal his handsome tanned face and pearly white teeth. He

moves and speaks with the sort of arrogant swagger that only money can bring. Indeed, he seems to have gold and silver flowing through his veins. What Douglas particularly brought to the role was an almost supernatural confidence, and, as a result, his Gecko is absolutely believable when, in a speech at a stockholders' meeting, he utters the film's most famous lines, based on the words of Ivan Boesky: "Greed is good. Greed works." But where the real-life raider was imprisoned for insider trading, Douglas won an Oscar for Best Actor.

In a departure from his average-guy roles, Michael Douglas played Gordon Gecko, the ruthless corporate raider of Oliver Stone's Wall Street, *and won an Oscar for his trouble.*

Wall Street
(1987)
Screenplay by Oliver Stone.
Produced by Edward K.
Pressman. Directed by
Oliver Stone.
(20th Century Fox) 124 m.

Playwright Edward Albee created in George and Martha, the protagonists of his groundbreaking *Who's Afraid of Virginia Woolf?*, a prototypical portrait of a couple coming apart at the seams. The emotional violence that they wreak

Most of Burton and Taylor's on-screen pairings were less than successful, but they scored a year after Virginia Woolf *as another battling couple, Petruchio and Katherine, in Franco Zeffirelli's buoyant version of* The Taming of the Shrew.

on one another and on a younger couple over one long night in a New England college town has a cumulative power that takes on apocalyptic proportions. For many people in

the 1960s, *Virginia Woolf?* was a portrait of the entire American middle-class in distress.

Albee wanted Bette Davis to play Martha and James Mason to play George (Uta Hagen and Arthur Hill had originated the roles on Broadway). It was producer Ernest Lehman, who also wrote the screen adaptation, who engaged Elizabeth Taylor, and she in turn suggested her husband, Richard Burton. Getting Burton and Taylor was something of a coup in that they were a

highly publicized couple off-screen, which added an extra dimension to

Richard Burton and Elizabeth Taylor made their best film together as George and Martha, the couple who engage in a prolonged emotional battle in the screen adaptation of Edward Albee's Who's Afraid of Virginia Woolf?. *Taylor won an Oscar for her powerhouse performance.*

VIRGINIA WOOLF?

their on-screen marriage. (For anyone who has ever seen *The Sandpiper* [1965], *Boom!* [1968], or any of their other

Burton and Taylor began their story relationship together when they made the lavish extravaganza Cleopatra *(1963). Taylor played the title role and Burton was Marc Antony.*

films together, it is easy to see why this is considered far and away their finest collaboration.)

Although Burton was disappointed with his work in the film, he gave a sharp, underrated performance as George, blunting his rugged good looks into a middle-aged seediness. However, Taylor's Martha was something else again. The 33-year-old actress fairly bulldozed her way through the movie, turning her usually girlish voice loud and shrill and her cover-

girl looks into those of a frowsy middle-aged harridan. Prodded by novice director Mike Nichols, Taylor gave an Oscar-winning performance, her second.

Who's Afraid of Virginia Woolf?
(1966)
Screenplay by Ernest Lehman, based on the play by Edward Albee. Produced by Ernest Lehman. Directed by Mike Nichols.
(Warner Bros.) 129 m.

COAL MINER'S DAUGHTER

For the role of country music singer Loretta Lynn, who went from the poverty of a Kentucky hollow to superstardom in a few dizzying years, Sissy Spacek matured in a little over two hours from a 13-year-old girl to a woman in her late 30s. That this metamorphosis was utterly believable is a tribute not only to an actress of Spacek's talent but also to her unique quality on screen. In every role, she seems forever on the brink of adulthood but never quite there, in possession of an almost otherworldly calm and poise that leaves her ageless.

Sissy Spacek as country singer Loretta Lynn, who worked her way up from poverty to the pinnacle of her profession, in Coal Miner's Daughter. *The actress' country singing was very credible and she accompanied herself on the guitar.*

But she did more than show Loretta aging in this rich role. Loretta begins the film as a naive young girl, married at 13 to a handsome ex-soldier Doolittle Lynn (Tommy Lee Jones) but terrified of sex (in one hilarious moment, she is disgusted by a sex manual he buys her). She grows into a caring mother and doting wife who finds her first successes singing in honky-tonks. After she's had a taste of stardom (under the tutelage of singing star Patsy Kline, played by Beverly D'Angelo), she becomes a wise older woman, scornful but indulgent of her husband's

One of Spacek's first leading roles was as the title character in Carrie, *the 1976 adaptation of Stephen King's novel about a backward teenager with telekinetic abilities. Here, after being drenched with pig's blood at the prom, she uses her powers to destroy her schoolmates.*

Coal Miner's Daughter
(1980)
Screenplay by Tom Rickman. Produced by Bob Larson. Directed by Michael Apted
(Universal) 124 m.

Spacek's role followed the Queen of Country Music from early adolescence into middle age, a metamorphosis that won her an Oscar. Here she is seen as a young girl in Butcher Holler, Kentucky.

another, she forgets the words to her own songs and must be prompted by her musicians.

In her Oscar-winning performance as the Queen of Country Music, Spacek did all her own singing and provided the guitar accompaniments, displaying, in addition to her bravura acting, musical skills that led her at one time to aspire to a career in country music. But, just as important, she projected an inner strength that gave the role backbone: her Loretta genuinely seemed rooted in the traditions and landscape of the Kentucky coal-mining country. One of the most memorable scenes in the film is the one in which Loretta sings in public for the first time, and the audience interest peaks. They, like the movie audience watching them, know they are seeing something special.

drinking and womanizing (she teaches him a lesson by writing a song about it). Finally, as a superstar, she falls apart, swamped by her own success. In one of the film's most harrowing moments, a fan rips a clump of hair from her head; in

Having starred in several box-office duds in a row during the late 1950s and early 1960s, Paul Newman found his career in a slump when he made *The Hustler*. He needed a hit, and he got one. Director Robert Rossen's version of the Walter Tevis novel about a lowlife pool hustler who takes on the great Minnesota Fats (Jackie Gleason) was a gripping look at a small subset of urban society, one

The Hustler
(1961)
Screenplay by Robert Rossen, based on the novel by Walter Tevis. Produced and directed by Robert Rossen.
(20th Century Fox) 135 m.

with which few moviegoers had any familiarity. But *The Hustler* conjured up, in spades, the atmosphere of seedy midwestern pool halls, and Newman, a trained method actor, fit right in. As Fast Eddie Felson, he looked like he had been hanging around for years. To prepare for the role, Newman worked with pool great Willie Mosconi, who did most of Eddie's trick shots for the film. And the actor used the elasticity of his body to great effect, making his and Mosconi's work with a cue especially convincing.

When not playing pool, Eddie is a loner, cocky on the outside but vulnerable beneath the surface. Finally, an embittered, slightly lame woman (Piper Laurie) gets to him and, without his realizing it, he falls in love. It is her suicide that gives him the cold hardness that he needs to finally beat Fats. It also gives him the fortitude to leave his parasitic stakehorse, Bert (George C. Scott). But he pays a terrible price for finding his decency. Bert forces him to leave the world of professional pool forever.

Newman had a firm grip on the emotional side of Eddie's life, handling well the hustler's flamboyance but tempering it with a wan smile. And, when he realizes that Bert has banned him from the game he loves, he reacts like a child who can't believe that he has to give up his favorite toy. Twenty-six years after *The Hustler*, Newman returned to the

Paul Newman gave one of the most compelling performances of his career in The Verdict *(1982). The sex symbol was not afraid to let all the warts show in his portrayal of an alcoholic Boston lawyer with only one client to his name.*

role, playing Eddie as a mellowed, wizened older man in *The Color of Money*. The result won him his first Oscar.

OPPOSITE: *Cocky, hardnosed Fast Eddie Felson (Paul Newman) learns about pool and life the hard way in* The Hustler. *The role, which Newman reprised 26 years later in* The Color of Money (1987), *was one of a number of antiheroic parts the actor played in the 1960s.*

F R A N K E N S T E I N

Director James Whale noticed Boris Karloff on the Universal lot when he was casting his 1931 adaptation of Mary Shelley's Frankenstein, and he knew he had his man. Tall, gaunt, and with haunted, sunken eyes, this British character actor was the soul of the monster.

Karloff and Whale's creation isn't very close to Shelley's rather genteel being. Rather, they created a huge, howling man-child. Part of the credit for the character's success goes to make-up man Jack Pierce, who designed the flat head, the pallid coloring, and the scar on the forehead. It took Karloff hours every day to get in and out of his make-up and costume, which included heavy leg braces to give him the stiff walk. But it was the actor who brought the monster to life. The result is a poignant figure, tormented by fire, longing for compassion. Of Karloff's three films in the role (later played without much success by Bela Lugosi, Lon Chaney, Jr., and Glenn Strange), the most enduring image comes from the first: the monster sitting by a river, innocently picking the petals off of flowers with a sweet and unsuspecting little girl, whom he then brutally murders in childlike frustration.

Boris Karloff is seen here in the role that defined his career, that of the monster in the 1931 version of Mary Shelley's Frankenstein.

> **Frankenstein**
> **(1931)**
> Scenario and dialogue by Garrett Fort and Francis Edward Faragoh, based on the novel by Mary Wollstonecraft Shelley. Directed by James Whale.
> (Universal) 71 m.

Sigourney Weaver as Ripley

ALIEN

To Sigourney Weaver the making of *Alien* was a horror, but this 1979 outer space variation of *Ten Little Indians* was the movie that made her career. It may have been unpleasant to film, but it was terrifying to watch, and she was its backbone.

Ripley is an officer aboard a ship traveling through deep space which answers a distress signal on a remote planet. What she and her crew find there is a life-form that is terror itself—a horrific, phallic creature that inhabits people, oozes a viscous gel, and grows at lightning speed (designed by artist H. R. Giger). Every member of the crew, including the captain, played by Tom Skerritt, is eventually killed off—except Ripley, who somehow manages to keep her wits about her.

Weaver is a statuesque beauty with seemingly perfect bone structure and refined, clipped speech. She projected a feeling of deep courage, strength, and intelligence in *Alien*, despite her horror over what she sees. A case in point is the now legendary scene in which another crew member, played by John Hurt, goes into a coughing fit, only to have an alien explode out of his stomach. Indeed, Ripley keeps her cool right up to the final moments when, as the lone survivor, she engages in a tense, final showdown with the alien.

Weaver's portrayal of Ripley set the standard for many tough futuristic heroines that followed (including Linda Hamilton in 1991's *Terminator 2*). She reprised the role in 1986 with *Aliens* and in 1992 with *Alien 3*.

Sigourney Weaver was strong-willed and courageous as Ripley, the only member of a spaceship crew to keep her wits about her in the stomach-churning sci-fi classic Alien. *Behind her is Ian Holm as the android, Ash.*

Alien
(1979)
Screenplay by Dan O'Bannon. Produced by Walter Hill, Gordon Carroll, and David Giler. Directed by Ridley Scott. (20th Century Fox) 117 m.

GENTLEMEN PREFER BLONDES

Nearly every director who worked with Marilyn Monroe commented upon how electric she was on camera and how ordinary she appeared otherwise. For example, Howard Hawks, who directed her in *Monkey Business* (1952) as well as in her signature role of Lorelei Lee in *Gentlemen Prefer Blondes*, once said, "She'd sit on the set with practically nothing on, and a pretty girl would walk by and ev-

ABOVE: *Perhaps the most celebrated image of Marilyn Monroe is this moment in* The Seven Year Itch *(1955), in which she stands on a subway grate to enjoy the breeze from the passing train below. Her apartment neighbor, played by co-star Tom Ewell, shares in her pleasure.*

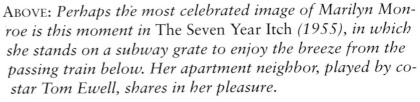

erybody'd whistle. But she got in front of the camera, and the camera liked her, and all of a sudden she was a great sex symbol."

Anita Loos' story of a "little girl from Little Rock" who goes digging for diamonds on a transatlantic cruise with her friend,

One of Monroe's best-remembered dramatic roles was that of a cafe singer being pursued by a rodeo cowboy, played by Don Murray, in the 1956 film version of William Inge's Bus Stop.

Dorothy (Jane Russell), had already been filmed as a silent in 1928 before Carol Channing made the role her own in the Broadway musical. Channing never registered on-screen the way Monroe did, though. Lorelei is a wonderful creation—a child in a woman's body, innocent of her own sexuality, firmly convinced that diamonds make the world go 'round. It was a perfect role for Monroe, who adopted a softer variation of Channing's clipped, comical way of speaking. Much of her charm, in ample abundance as Lorelei, comes from how relaxed she is, a looseness that threatens to disintegrate into chaos but never quite does, a skyrocket just before it burns out. For the big, standout production number, "Diamonds Are a Girl's Best Friend," Monroe demonstrated her ability with a song, revealing a sharpness and flash.

Marilyn Monroe shows off her assets as Lorelei Lee, the "little girl from Little Rock" in the film based on the Broadway musical Gentlemen Prefer Blondes.

Gentlemen Prefer Blondes
(1953)
Screenplay by Charles Lederer, based on the musical by Anita Loos and Joseph Fields. Songs by Hoagy Carmichael and Harold Adamson, and Jule Styne and Leo Robin Produced by Sol C. Siegel. Directed by Howard Hawks.
(20th Century Fox) 91 m.

In his heyday, John Barrymore was known as "the Great Profile" and, in keeping with this sobriquet, demanded that he be photographed only from the left side. The most famous member of an American acting dynasty, he came to the movies after winning renown on the New York stage. He did become a great romantic star of the silents, but by the early 1930s, his career was well past its peak. Drinking and mercurial behavior had taken their toll. But if his status as a matinee idol was in jeopardy, it did not affect the

Twentieth Century
(1934)
Screenplay by Ben Hecht and Charles MacArthur, based on their play. Directed by Howard Hawks. (Columbia) 91 m.

quality of his acting. He gave some of his most memorable performances in the twilight of his career and at the end of his life (he would be dead by 1942). Among them was Oscar Jaffe in *Twentieth Century.*

"It's the story of the greatest ham in the world, and God knows you fit that," director Howard Hawks told Barrymore when he asked him to play the part. Once Barrymore had signed on, Hawks and writers Ben Hecht and Charles MacArthur tailored the role to fit his temperamental personality and still-athletic mien. As actor/impresario Jaffe, he leaps, flails, and ca-

vorts around the screen, dishes out orders to his minions (Walter Connolly and Roscoe Karns) in flowing tones, and shamelessly schemes to lure his equally hammy leading lady, Lily Garland (a feisty, young Carole Lombard), back into his fold. The beauty of Barrymore's performance lay in his self-awareness: he seemed to have had an uncanny understanding of the depths of an actor's vanity, of the almost constant need of flattering attention. The irony is that Barrymore put aside his own vanity to put on film this comic expression of egotism incarnate.

The role of Broadway actor/impresario Oscar Jaffe in Twentieth Century *was tailored specifically to fit the temperament of leading man John Barrymore, seen here with his equally hammy leading lady, Lily Garland (Carole Lombard).*

In his Oscar-winning role as Popeye Doyle in The French Connection, *Gene Hackman plays a scrappy New York cop who chases down a cache of heroin.*

Gene Hackman was a New York character actor who made his way into *Bonnie and Clyde* (1967), for which he won an Oscar nomination. He was scared to death when he was tapped by director William Friedkin to play the lead in *The French Connection.* Friedkin was after a quality far grittier than anything the big stars of the day could give him (early candidates for the role were Jackie Gleason and Jimmy Breslin!) and so he chose the 40-year-old newcomer. It seems odd in retrospect that this most reliable of leading men was terrified about his ability to carry the film, for in the end it made him a star and won him an Oscar for Best Actor.

Hackman saw the part of Popeye, who was based on real-life New York detective Eddie Egan, as kin to the Cagney characters of the 1930s: tough, wise-cracking, and right from the street. His detective on the trail of a major drug shipment, decked out in a porkpie hat and dirty raincoat, is certainly all of those things, but he is also possessed of a lethally obsessive edge that makes him as dangerous as the suave French heroin trafficker (Fernando Rey) he is tracking. In one of the film's most memorable moments, one can almost feel Popeye's murderous exasperation as the drug kingpin waves to him from the protection of a departing subway car. In another, Popeye drives at top speed in pursuit of his prey under a Queens El, almost heedless of pedestrians. Incidentally, for this, the film's most terrifying sequence, Hackman did quite a bit of his own driving.

Hackman reprised the role of Popeye in the 1975 sequel, set in Marseilles. It featured a long, draining sequence in which the detective goes cold turkey to kick a heroin addiction forced on him by his captors.

The French Connection
(1971)
Screenplay by Ernest Tidyman, based on the book by Robin Moore. Produced by Philip D'Antoni. Directed by William Friedkin.
(20th Century Fox) 104 m.

The team of Astaire and . . . Dorothy Jordan? Who? Ms. Jordan is the actress who almost played the dancing partner of Broadway star Fred Astaire in his 1933 film debut, *Flying Down to Rio,* but she decided to get married instead. Her replacement was Ginger Rogers, primarily known at that time as a pretty, wisecracking comedienne.

Pairing Astaire with Rogers was perhaps the movies' most magical cou-

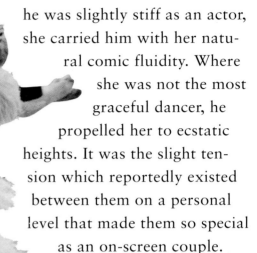

pling. The pair worked so well throughout their many films together in part because their relationship seemed a bit improbable. He was urbane, graceful, and slightly brittle, while she was tough, earthy, and sexy. But each made up for the other's shortcomings beautifully. Where

he was slightly stiff as an actor, she carried him with her natural comic fluidity. Where she was not the most graceful dancer, he propelled her to ecstatic heights. It was the slight tension which reportedly existed between them on a personal level that made them so special as an on-screen couple.

Most of their films together had the same sweet romantic complications, and in this one they are kept apart by a case of mistaken iden-

RIGHT: *Fred Astaire and Ginger Rogers as Josh and Dinah Barkley in their tenth and final screen appearance together,* The Barkleys of Broadway *(1949).*

80

tity. If *Top Hat* has become the most enduring of their collaborations, it is probably because in its extreme stylization it creates a wonderful, private little world that seems to exist only for Jerry and Dale, especially as they glide across the dance floor to "Cheek to Cheek." But in all their films together, Astaire and Rogers were serendipity incarnate.

Top Hat
(1935)
Screenplay by Dwight Taylor and Allan Scott, based on the musical *The Gay Divorcee* by Dwight Taylor and a play by Alexander Farago and Aladar Laszlo. Produced by Pandro S. Berman. Directed by Mark Sandrich.
(RKO) 100 m.

LEFT AND OPPOSITE, ABOVE AND FAR LEFT: *The grace and style of Hollywood's most celebrated dance couple, Fred Astaire and Ginger Rogers, is evident in this sequence of photos from their fourth and most famous film,* Top Hat.

81

Paramount asked virtually every young actor in Hollywood to read for the part of Michael Corleone, war hero and the youngest son of a Mafia chieftain who goes against his father's wishes and becomes involved with the family "business." And with every new batch of screen tests that director Francis Ford Coppola was forced to shoot, he would slip in a new one of Al Pacino, so convinced was he that the young actor was ideally suited to the role. After Coppola prevailed and the film was under way, studio executives still ago-

> **The Godfather**
> (1972)
> Screenplay by Francis Ford Coppola and Mario Puzo, based on the novel by Mario Puzo. Produced by Albert S. Ruddy. Directed by Francis Ford Coppola.
> (Paramount) 175 m.

nized over the decision, finding Pacino ordinary and unexpressive. They were ready to replace both the actor and his director at a moment's notice. Then came the restaurant scene, in which Michael vengefully guns down the men who tried to kill his father (Sterling Hayden and Al Lettieri). The way Pacino slowly built up his character's tension in that scene was ample proof of his ability to carry the film's pivotal role.

It is appropriate that the restaurant scene was the turning point for Pacino, a young New York actor with only a few credits to his name, because the murder is also the turning point for Michael. Thereafter he progresses from a clean-cut American boy to an avenging son to a murderous Mafia patriarch whose authority grows as his capacity for love diminishes. It is exciting for a lover of film acting to watch how Pacino effected these changes. The rhythm of his character be-

In a dramatic departure from the lonely, murderous Michael Corleone, Pacino brought great patience and tenderness to his role as Johnny, a short-order cook who adores waitress Frankie (Michelle Pfeiffer), in Frankie and Johnny *(1991).*

*Pacino had his first post-*Godfather *triumph in the 1975 movie* Dog Day Afternoon, *based on the true story of two bumbling Brooklyn robbers who hold a bank under siege one long, sweltering summer day.*

comes slower, more regal, as the epic progresses, and the weight of his presence is felt more and more keenly. When he finally outbursts are shocking, and his lonely moments of reflection shattering.

In *The Godfather, Part III* which helped make perceptible his need to unfasten the chains of his past. Pacino has been memorable in plenty of other

During the course of Francis Ford Coppola's epic film, The Godfather, *Al Pacino as Michael Corleone progresses from a clean-cut American boy, to an avenging son, to a murderous Mafia patriarch. Seen here at the movie's end, he is every inch the emotionless master of all he surveys.*

reaches the pinnacle of his power in The *Godfather, Part II,* Michael's ability to calmly and dispassionately discuss murder is appalling, his sudden (1990), when Michael Corleone has retired from the Mafia to become a powerful legitimate businessman, Pacino found a certain lightness to the character films, but he has made his deepest and most lasting mark as Michael Corleone. It seems odd to think that once he was considered wrong for the part.

Henry Fonda's Tom Joad has become a central piece of film Americana, a symbol of the

common man if ever there was one. He has become so identified with the role that it seems remarkable now that other actors were even considered for it. Don Ameche or Tyrone Power as Tom? At one time they were strong possibilities. Given the film's source material and the fact that it was directed by John Ford, it might have still been powerful with Power or

Henry Fonda took seven years off from the movies to appear on the Broadway stage in the title role of the 1948 hit Mister Roberts. *He returned to Hollywood for the 1955 film version and is pictured here with James Cagney as his irascible ship's captain.*

Ameche, but it is doubtful that either of them could have imbued the destitute Okie farmer with the dignity or righteous

For his final role, as Norman Thayer in On Golden Pond *(1981), Henry Fonda finally won the Oscar for Best Actor that had eluded him throughout his career. He also had the chance to work for the first time with Katharine Hepburn, who played his wife.*

conviction that so elevated the character as played by Fonda.

There was a sad quality to Henry Fonda's persona dur-

The Grapes of Wrath
(1940)
Screenplay by Nunnally Johnson, based on the novel by John Steinbeck. Produced by Darryl F. Zanuck. Directed by John Ford.
(20th Century Fox) 129 m.

ing the early part of his career. Life seemed to weigh heavily on his shoulders, suggested by his famous slow, deliberate gait and twangy Midwestern speech pattern. What would appear statesmanlike in later years seemed tragic in his youth. That quality served him particularly well in *The Grapes of Wrath*, where he had to embody a destitute farmer whose family is

Looking at the bleak, anguished expression on Henry Fonda's face in this photo from The Grapes of Wrath *reminds one of all the images of Oklahoma dust bowl victims taken during the Depression. Fonda's Tom Joad was a powerful evocation of the spirit and dignity of the common man.*

cast adrift by drought, economic depression, and insensitive bureaucrats. Thanks to Fonda, Tom's honesty, his goodness, and his faith are unquestionable and rock solid, evident from his first appearance in the film, a lanky figure in overalls and cap.

The actor was at his best during his touching exchanges with Jane Darwell who played Tom's beloved mother, and never more so than in the famous scene near the end of the film when Tom parts from his family, saying, "Wherever there's a fight so hungry people can eat, I'll be there. Wherever there's a cop beating up a guy, I'll be there. And when our people eat the stuff they raise, and live in the houses they build, why, I'll be there, too."

According to Gene Kelly, the actual "Singin' in the Rain" production number was the easiest thing that he did on the film, either as a dancer or a co-director. The most difficult thing about it was to control all that water. Which is proof that magic and complexity have nothing to do with one another.

This classic production number is one of Hollywood's great moments, made possible by one of its two greatest dancers. But where Fred Astaire was controlled and elegant and worked best with a partner,

Kelly was exuberant and self-assured, with an athletic physique and an all-American smile, and had his greatest moments alone. "Singin' in the Rain" or "I Like Myself," the dance on roller skates from *It's Always Fair Weather* (1955), are raptures in which Kelly's characters express physically the sheer joy of being in love. Aside from the title number, there are a host of other wonderful moments in *Singin' in the Rain,* particularly those that involve Kelly and Jean Hagen as silent film stars struggling with the advent of sound. There are plenty of other great production numbers as well: "Moses Supposes," Kelly's duet with Donald O'Connor, and the lavish "Broadway Melody" with Kelly and Cyd Charisse, to name two. But it is Kelly alone, twirling his umbrella, climbing a lamppost, merrily splashing in puddles, and happily shrugging at a passing cop on the beat that remain the film's most potent images.

Singin' in the Rain
(1952)
Story and screenplay by Adolph Green and Betty Comden. Produced by Arthur Freed. Directed by Stanley Donen and Gene Kelly.
(MGM) 102 m.

Gene Kelly as Don Lockwood lets his cares wash away in the title number from Singin' In the Rain, *one of the most memorable sequences in the history of the Hollywood musical.*

J ill Clayburgh all but vanished from the movies in the early 1980s. Perhaps her disappearance was only fitting, since her film persona was so completely attached to the 1970s. Indeed, during the days of smile buttons, pet rocks, and Jimmy Carter, Jill Clayburgh was the toast of Hollywood. She is a gutsy actress who took on interesting projects during her brief tenure as a star (no further proof is needed than her performance in 1979's *Luna,* about an incestuous relationship between a mother and her son). But the role with which she will always be identified is Erica, the abandoned wife who slowly finds her identity in Paul Mazursky's *An Unmarried Woman.*

Millions of women identified with the horror and fear that Jill Clayburgh as Erica felt in An Unmarried Woman *when her husband told her that he was leaving her. This housewife's journey into self-actualization made her an icon of her age.*

Clayburgh is adept at playing shy women with hidden wellsprings of emotion, hinted at with hesitant body language and a gently quavering voice. The most memorable moments in the film center around Erica's rushes of feeling: her uncomprehending reaction when her husband (Michael Murphy) tells her that he wants a divorce; her improvised ballet performance in the freedom of her apartment; her sudden, mad rush to eliminate every reminder of her husband from her home in the middle of the night.

The freedom that Erica haltingly but decidedly embraces in *An Unmarried Woman* made her an icon of her age, although the ending of the film was hotly debated at the time, with many people feeling that Erica was nuts to cling to her independence and forgo her relationship with Alan Bates' dashing artist, Saul. It was Clayburgh's grace, unusual beauty, and enormous ability to funnel emotion through a role that brought this intriguing character to vivid life.

An Unmarried Woman
(1978)
Screenplay by Paul Mazursky. Produced by Paul Mazursky and Tony Ray. Directed by Paul Mazursky.
(20th Century Fox) 124 m.

ROMAN HOLIDAY

Roman Holiday marked the American screen debut of a 23-year-old actress named Audrey Hepburn, and she enchanted everyone right off the bat. Hepburn looked like a real princess wandering through Rome on a lark in this Cinderella-story-in-reverse, in which a princess who is trapped by her royal duties longs to be a regular citizen. With her refined accent and lyrical vocal intonations, her swan-like neck, gamine physique, doe-like eyes, and decorous manner, Hepburn was the very picture of royalty, and she

Audrey Hepburn won an Oscar for her debut performance as a princess who runs away from her duties and falls in love with a reporter (Gregory Peck) in Roman Holiday.

Roman Holiday
(1953)
Screenplay by Ian McLellan Hunter and John Dighton, based on a story by Hunter. Produced and directed by William Wyler.
(Paramount) 119 m.

waltzed off with the Oscar for Best Actress in 1953.

As it happened, Hepburn's first Hollywood film nearly didn't come off because director William Wyler was prevented, for budgetary reasons, from shooting in Rome. Eventually he was given the choice of filming on location in black-and-white or shooting on the Paramount lot in color, and he opted for

Rome, still in disarray after World War II. Although he had some trouble obtaining permits from the Italian government, the shoot eventually proved to be a pleasant experience.

Hepburn's co-star was Gregory Peck as Joe Bradley, the hard-bitten reporter with whom the princess falls in love. He was initially resistant to playing the role, but he was won over by his young co-star, and in the end they worked wonderfully together. Peck's solidity seemed like an anchor for her lightness. But everyone concerned knew that this was Hepburn's movie from start to

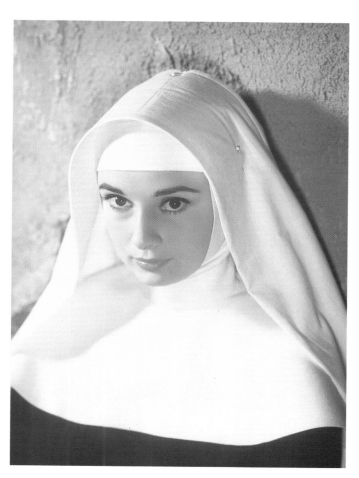

Hepburn received another Oscar nomination for her portrayal of a young Belgian woman who joins a strict religious order and is sent as a missionary to the Congo in The Nun's Story *(1959).*

finish. From the opening moments of the film, a short newsreel and a ball in which the princess must dance with one ancient dignitary after another, Hepburn all but announces herself as a major new screen presence.

In a departure from the somewhat naive, introverted characters she usually played, Hepburn took on the role of Truman Capote's eccentric, flamboyant party girl, Holly Golightly, in Breakfast at Tiffany's *(1961).*

FUNNY GIRL

Barbra Streisand first garnered acclaim on Broadway with a supporting role in the musical called *I Can Get It for You Wholesale,* in which she stole the show singing a tune called "Miss Marmelstein." At 22, she became a star in *Funny Girl,* the musical biography of the great Ziegfeld comedienne Fanny Brice.

Streisand announced herself as a new star in no uncertain terms: her unusual looks, her tremendously powerful singing voice, her assured presence, and her talent spoke for themselves. When Hollywood beckoned, it did so in a big way, offering her a three-picture deal without even so much as a screen test. Barbra Streisand ruled Hollywood before she even arrived there.

Funny Girl was given lavish treatment in its transition from stage to screen: sumptuous sets, veteran director William Wyler in charge, and, as Brice's husband, the unfortunate gambler Nicky Arnstein, no less a leading man than Omar Sharif, with whom Streisand reportedly had an affair during filming. Rumors of Streisand's dictatorial behavior on the set spread even in this, her maiden voyage in the movies. But even those who disliked her agreed that she was a knockout on-screen. She was absolutely perfect for the role of a homely Jewish girl from New York who works her way to stardom with talent and chutzpah—art certainly imitated life there—and what the filmmakers did best was give her ample opportunity to display her bigger-than-life talents. The show-stopper is the musical number "Don't Rain on My Parade," which takes Fanny soaring through New York on all manner of transportation as Streisand's voice soared to match.

Funny Girl
(1968)
Screenplay by Isobel Lennart, from her libretto. Music by Jule Styne, lyrics by Bob Merrill. Produced by Ray Stark. Directed by William Wyler.
(Columbia) 169 m.

Barbra Streisand made her film debut as vaudeville star Fanny Brice in Funny Girl, *and her powerhouse re-creation of her triumphant Broadway performance earned her an Oscar. She returned to the role for the not-as-successful sequel,* Funny Lady, *in 1975.*

ROAD TO SINGAPORE

Bob Hope and Bing Crosby were radio stars who solidified their careers in films when they were cast together for the first time in *Road to Singapore*. This was the start of one of the most popular film series ever, ending more than 20 years later with *The Road to Hong Kong* (1962).

Hope and Crosby may have been the most relaxed,

cally playing the charming rogue to Hope's nervous nebbish. Indeed, the *Road* films, leisurely, low-key romps all, were built around the personalities of the stars. In each, Crosby's character gets into some kind of a jam, and he and the Hope character escape to some faraway place together. There they meet a woman

In each of their outings together, Hope's frenetic nerves and fast-paced talk (Woody Allen has often cited him as a model for his own work) wonderfully complimented Der Bingle's easy confidence and almost lackadaisical acting style. In *Singapore*, for example, Hope's Ace is forever fidgeting over some jam Crosby's Josh, a wealthy and irresponsible youth, has gotten the two of them into. Josh, of course, remains the model of calm. There are pleasant song interludes, and perhaps the funniest moment comes when Ace and Josh, trying to freeload a meal, disguise themselves as natives and join Lamour's Mima at a Singaporean cookout.

Crooner Bing Crosby (right) *and comedian Bob Hope pooled their impressive talents in a series of Road pictures that extended for more than 20 years. The relaxed, light-hearted attitudes of the stars, evident in this publicity still for the first picture,* The Road to Singapore, *contributed mightily to the popularity of the series. Seen with them here is Dorothy Lamour, who co-starred in all seven films.*

> **Road to Singapore**
> (1940)
> Screenplay by Don Hartman and Frank Butler, based on a story by Harry Hervey. Produced by Harlan Thompson. Directed by Victor Schertzinger.
> (Paramount) 84 m.

jovial comedy team ever to appear in movies, with Bing typically

played by Dorothy Lamour and good-naturedly fight over her.

Marion Morrison began his film career as a set decorator on a 1920 silent movie called *Mother Machree*, directed by John Ford. In time, he worked his way into acting and had his first starring role in the 1930 Western epic *The Big Trail*, for which he acquired the name John Wayne. The rest of the decade found him in countless grade-Z Westerns before Ford, who had become a friend, cast him in the lead of his 1939 classic, *Stagecoach*. This was the first film in a collaboration that lasted for four decades. The eight Westerns that Wayne made with Ford virtually define the genre. In fact, it is difficult to imagine the Western without them. The apex of their collaboration came in 1956 with *The Searchers*.

Wayne felt that *The Searchers* was his crowning achievement—he even named a son after his character. Far from a simple Western good guy, Ethan is a complex individual, heroic but prejudiced against Indians, lonely yet only able to live alone and bitter (Ethan's cynical repetition of the line, "That'll be the day," was the inspiration for the Buddy Holly song). He and Martin Pawley (Jeffrey Hunter) spend years and cross thousands of miles from Arizona to Canada tracking Debbie (Natalie Wood), his niece who was kidnapped in an Indian raid when she was very young. When he finds her, dressed as a squaw, his hatred of the Comanches is so great that he wants to shoot her, but instead he picks her up in a grand motion and takes her home. In the end, he leaves the family he has spent his life searching for and walks back into the desert alone.

The absolute authority

> **The Searchers**
> **(1956)**
> Screenplay by Frank S. Nugent, based on the novel by Alan LeMay. Produced by Merian C. Cooper and Patrick Ford. Directed by John Ford. (Republic) 119 m.

In John Ford's The Searchers, *John Wayne played the complex role of Ethan Edwards, the bitter, lonely, Indian-hating ex-Confederate soldier who spends years tracking his niece, Debbie (Natalie Wood), across the Western landscape. Wayne considered his performance in the film his crowning achievement.*

Long before the end of his career, Wayne had become an integral part of the nation's culture. Here, he plays another of his typically American roles as a World War II marine in Sands of Iwo Jima *(1949).*

with which Wayne played Ethan was enough to quiet all those who maintained over the years that he couldn't act. But

there were also moments of deep emotion in this role, and Wayne realized them beautifully—his unspeakable sadness when he finds the body of his other niece, for example, or the bitterness that creases his face when he sees two young girls driven mad by their Indian captivity. Wayne never had to be an Olivier. He was completely

As the aging one-eyed marshal, Rooster Cockburn, John Wayne prepares to square off against a band of outlaws, guiding his horse with the reins in his mouth. For his performance in True Grit *(1969), the veteran film actor finally won an Oscar.*

at home against the American landscape, and his film roles made him an integral part of the nation's culture. He was John Wayne, and that was more than good enough.

Wayne played an American boxer who moves to Ireland in the uproarious The Quiet Man *(1952), one of his few non-Western collaborations with his good friend, director John Ford. He is pictured here with Maureen O'Hara as the woman he courts and fights for in the classic scene that ends the movie.*

Julia Roberts as Vivian Ward

PRETTY WOMAN

As written, the role of Vivian in the film *Pretty Woman* is a proverbial "hooker with a heart of gold"; she just wants what everyone else wants—to love and be loved. Only an actress with the kind of freshness, vivacity, and sex appeal of a Julia Roberts could have breathed genuine life into the role. As the L. A. streetwalker who lucks her way into a week in a Beverly Hills hotel with a handsome millionaire corporate raider named Edward Lewis (Richard Gere), she made audiences believe this good, old-fashioned fairy tale. And why not? Her Vivian could charm the birds off the trees.

Roberts brought a conviction to her role as well as a disarming spontaneity. Many of her most memorable moments onscreen—Vivian's hurt and embarrassment when she is scoffed at by Rodeo Drive salespeople, her

awkwardness at a business dinner as she pretends to be Lewis' girlfriend, and her joy when Lewis flies her to San Francisco for her first opera—had an unaffected naturalness. The childlike innocence and gawkiness (as in the hilarious moment when she can't figure out how to work a pair of opera glasses) and the ab-

solute candor did not seem like a performance at

all, but to flow effortlessly from one who actually possesses those qualities. And her exchanges with Gere, who brought just the right emotional reserve to his role, were wonderful. At times, Vivian is like a mother to him. At other times, she is like a real Cinderella to his Prince. Near the end, when even the hardened hotel manager (Hector Elizondo) hopes that they will stay together, one can't help but hope too, despite all logic to the contrary. While Gere certainly helped make rooters out of audiences everywhere, it was ultimately Roberts who brought the magic to what might otherwise have been a run-of-the-mill movie.

The charismatic Julia Roberts shot to stardom as Vivian, the Los Angeles streetwalker who becomes a Beverly Hills Cinderella in Pretty Woman.

Pretty Woman
(1990)
Screenplay by J. F. Lawton. Produced by Arnon Milchan and Stephen Reuther. Directed by Garry Marshall.
(Touchstone) 117 m.

For the first sound version of the popular Edgar Rice Burroughs novel, *Tarzan of the Apes*, MGM initially cast actor Bruce Bennett, who then became unavailable due to an injury. His replacement was Olympic gold medalist Johnny Weissmuller, in his first starring role. Burroughs never cared much for Weissmuller's portrayal of the jungle boy raised by and among apes. But this lean, athletic Tarzan became the definitive one, with Weissmuller appearing in 11 Tarzan films altogether, six with the charming Maureen O'Sullivan as Jane.

Recognizing that he was no actor, Weissmuller modestly attributed his success in the role to his ability to grunt properly (someone else dubbed in the holler). But it was his solid physique, amply displayed in a loincloth, that made the real impression. He certainly didn't look like he had been raised in the jungle, but realism was never what drew audiences to the films. In the first of the series, it was sex appeal. O'Sullivan was beguilingly pretty and uninhibited as

In 1932 Olympic gold medalist Johnny Weissmuller was cast in his first leading role, as Tarzan in Tarzan, the Ape Man. *He would continue as the jungle hero in 10 more films, six of which also featured Maureen O'Sullivan, pictured here, as Jane.*

Jane, and she and Weissmuller made a very appealing couple.

As the years went by, the

Tarzan the Ape Man
(1932)
Scenario by Cyril Hume, dialogue by Ivor Novello, based on characters created by Edgar Rice Burroughs. Directed by W. S. Van Dyke
(MGM) 99 m.

---

films in the series became cheaper and more formulaic, and by the time Weissmuller retired from the role in 1948 and Lex Barker took over, he had became so associated with Tarzan in the public mind that he went directly into the similar *Jungle Jim* series. In the last of those films, he gave up the ghost and played a character named . . . Johnny Weissmuller.

❦ LITTLE CAESAR ❦

Edward G. Robinson was a New York stage actor with no intention of going into films. When he had a Broadway hit with *The Racket* in 1923, however, Hollywood beckoned, and the money was good. What was intended as a short stay lasted throughout a long and fruitful career. By 1930, Robinson had changed his tune about the movies, and he talked his way into the lead of his breakthrough film. He was originally cast in a small role in *Little Caesar,* but it isn't hard to imagine how the force of his personality could sway the executives at Warner Brothers into rethinking their choice for the lead, in much the same way that Rico's undeniable willpower makes him king of the rackets.

Robinson's kingpin, patterned after Al Capone, was the first of the gangster prototypes, quickly followed by James Cagney in *The Public Enemy* (1931) and Paul Muni in *Scarface* (1932). But the original was perhaps the most psychologically complex. As opposed to Cagney's bantam grace and agility or Muni's ape-like posturing, Robinson was most effective when standing stock still, letting his bulldog snarl speak for itself,

> **Little Caesar**
> (1930)
> Screenplay by Francis Faragoh and Robert E. Lee, based on the novel by W. R. Burnett. Directed by Mervyn LeRoy.
> (Warner Bros.) 77 m.

Veteran stage actor Edward G. Robinson achieved stardom as Enrico Bandello, a vicious, snarling gangster, patterned after Al Capone, in Little Caesar. *It quickly became the model for subsequent roles played by the likes of James Cagney and George Raft.*

barking orders in his famous staccato growl. He was particularly adept at conveying Rico the megalomaniac, the man who is totally enamored of the fancy trappings of power. Indeed, Robinson keyed into the character's madness in the film's final scenes when Rico, destitute and on the lam in a flea-bitten flophouse, still envisions himself as the lord of the mobs. Never was he more effective than in the film's final moment when Rico lies riddled with bullets, and he delivers his famous last line with blunt astonishment: "Mother of mercy—is this the end of Rico?" The genteel Robinson played gangsters throughout his long career, and *Little Caesar,* created in his youth, was his ticket to film success, but it also became the basis for many years of unhappy typecasting.

Yul Brynner as King Monghut

Has there ever been an actor so completely, so thoroughly identified with a role as Yul Brynner is with the King of Siam in *The King and I*? Has any actor ever played a role for so much of his career? Brynner originated the part on Broadway, re-created it in the film, reprised it later in his career on Broadway, and even did a short-lived television series based on the show. To say that he played it well does not do him justice. He owned it. So much so that an account of the remainder of his film career reads like a series of footnotes to his appearances as the King. Of course, Brynner's bald head and Eurasian features did not lend themselves to a great variety of roles. It is probably safe to say that, with the exception of a few diehard sci-fi fans who could cite his appearance as the robot in *Westworld* (1973) or Western fans who remember him in *The Magnificent Seven* (1960), Brynner is the King to all.

It may come as a surprise, then, to learn that he was initially reluctant to play the part on the screen. He was so protective of the property (the Rodgers and Hammerstein musical was based

---

The King and I
(1956)
Screenplay by Ernest Lehman, based on the musical by Richard Rodgers and Oscar Hammerstein II, from the book Anna and the King of Siam by Margaret Landon. Produced by Charles Brackett. Directed by Walter Lang.
(20th Century Fox) 133 m.

---

on the actual experiences of Margaret Landon, and her book had already served as the basis for the 1949 non-musical *Anna and the King of Siam*, with Rex Harrison) that he wanted to produce the film with Marlon Brando as the king.

The movie did not hide its stage origins well, but it was filled with color and pageantry. Deborah Kerr was delightful as Anna, but ultimately it was Brynner's film. He conveyed the ritualized stateliness that is traditional in portrayals of monarchs, but he added a childlike sense of wonder, translating what Anna tells him of the West into terms that he can understand, and adopting in the process the phrase, "Et cetera, et cetera, et cetera," that she casually uses once in conversation. He also brought to the role a physical, almost sensual power and grace that culminated in the celebrated "Shall We Dance" sequence. Hands on hips, legs spread apart, his King is imperious yet charming—when introducing his slew of children and wives to an incredulous Anna and when asking her to take a letter while reclining so that he can lie down. ("No one's head can be higher than King's!") Not surprisingly, this vital performance won Brynner his only Oscar.

Yul Brynner in the role he played virtually throughout his career, the magisterial King of Siam, in the film version of the Broadway musical smash, The King and I.

NORMA RAE

Harriet Frank and Irving Ravetch's screenplay for *Norma Rae* was based on the life of a real North Carolina mill worker, and the unvarnished, everyday quality of the role left many actresses uninterested. So the filmmakers took a chance on Sally Field, who had been known up to that point as television's *Flying Nun,* and was eager to gain respectability.

Field may never live down her infamous, fawning exclamation "You like me!" when she won an Oscar for *Places in the Heart* (1984), but her work in *Norma Rae,* for which she won her first Academy Award, was proof positive of her talent and

remains so. As the uneducated textile worker who becomes a gutsy union advocate under the tutelage of a northern organizer named Reuben Warshovski (Ron Leibman), Field seemed to give it her all. From her pitch perfect southern accent to her authentically blue collar look to her enormous emotional investment in the role, her Norma was an inspiring creation. She was right up there with James Stewart's Mr. Smith as a populist hero, and the fact that, along the way, she learns about poetry, opera, and a world outside of her existence makes her all the more touching. What might have been a one-dimensional, impossibly good

Norma Rae
(1979)
Screenplay by Harriet Frank and Irving Ravetch. Produced and directed by Martin Ritt.
(20th Century Fox) 114 m.

LEFT: *Field may never live down her infamous, fawning exclamation "You like me!" when she won an Oscar for her role as a widowed farm owner who brings her cotton crop to market with the help of a drifter named Mose (Danny Glover) in* Places in the Heart *(1984).*

OPPOSITE: *Sally Field achieved respectability as an actress playing a gutsy southern textile worker who fights to unionize her mill in* Norma Rae.

stereotype on paper became a flesh-and-blood character in Field's hands. There is not a hint of glamour or narcissism in her acting. When Norma shows her children photographs of their various fathers, when she subtly flirts with Reuben—it seems to come naturally to her—or, in the film's most moving scene, when she stands up with a union sign and inspires a work shutdown, she seems to be a real, honest-to-goodness human being.

MY FAIR LADY

For the lavish film version of Lerner and Loewe's smash Broadway musical, *My Fair Lady,* Warner Brothers decided to play it safe and go with an established

My Fair Lady
(1964)
Screenplay by Alan Jay Lerner, based on the musical by Lerner and Frederick Loewe and the play *Pygmalion* by George Bernard Shaw. Produced by Jack L. Warner. Directed by George Cukor.
(Warner Bros.) 170 m.

screen star for the role of Eliza Doolittle, the cocky waif transformed into a Victorian lady on a bet. The casting of Audrey Hepburn over Julie Andrews, who originated the role on stage, was a controversial and much-criticized decision. Peter O'Toole was the first choice to play Eliza's mentor and Svengali, Professor Henry Higgins. Cary Grant was also sought, and his reply was that Warners should "quit the foolishness and hire Rex Harrison." This was sound advice indeed. *My Fair Lady* without Rex Harrison? Unthinkable.

Harrison's Higgins is a confident, dashing gentleman, played with the actor's customary mixture of imperiousness and devilish charm, a true lord of the manor. Adding to the magic of the character of the original play by George Bernard Shaw are the musical numbers, which Harrison delivered in his unique style, a sort of rhythmic speech, at once lilting and precise. With his supremely elegant diction, the polished actor caught the spirit of the self-satisfied Edwardian bachelor perfectly, as in his beautiful rendering of the song "A Hymn to Him," in which he blithely asks, "Would I run off and never tell me where I'm going?/Well, why can't a woman be like me?" Director George Cukor did something unusual for Harrison's wonderful musical numbers, including "I've Grown Accus-

In the opening scene of My Fair Lady, *Professor Henry Higgins (Rex Harrison) pontificates on the particularities of English accents, region by region. His rendition of the song, "Why Can't the English" was delivered in a kind of rhythmic lilt that was uniquely and charmingly his.*

tomed to Her Face" and the infectious "The Rain in Spain." Rather than post-dubbing, which is customary in musicals, he recorded Harrison's voice directly with a concealed microphone to preserve the unique mixture of exactness and spontaneity.

James Dean has become an American legend. Bookstores abound with literary tributes and monographs, and his image—pompadour, baby face with half-smile/half-scowl, T-shirt, and jeans—seems to be everywhere. Much of the fascination certainly comes from the tangle between the real Dean and his screen persona. His life appears to have been as tortured as the performances he gave, and his death neatly perpetuated for all time his youthful rebellion on and off screen. It was as if he refused to grow old or to tarnish his reputation with any of the mediocre films that would have inevitably come his way had he lived. Except for a few tiny walk-ons and some television roles, he left film fans with only three performances. And of these, his Jim in *Rebel Without a Cause* was his most passionate and his most emblematic. Perhaps the role of the young man who only wants to be understood touched him the most deeply.

Rebel Without a Cause
(1955)
Screenplay by Stewart Stern, from a story by Nicholas Ray. Produced by David Weisbart. Directed by Nicholas Ray.
(Warner Bros.) 111 m.

Director Nicholas Ray knew that he couldn't treat Dean like an ordinary actor. Many of his moments in the film were improvised, including the famous scene in which Jim cools his forehead with a bottle of milk from the refrigerator (the set design for the kitchen was based on the one in Ray's home, where the improvisational work was done).

Jim is a prototypically alienated adolescent, trying to build a private world with his friends (Sal Mineo and Natalie Wood) because he cannot find a common language with his parents. It is a story that has been done to death since 1955, but out of all those offerings it is difficult to think of an actor who has come close to Dean's conviction in the role. The seemingly reckless physical abandon of his acting made

him unique among screen performers. Jim's exchanges with his obtuse but well-meaning father (Jim Backus) are probably the most poignant moments in *Rebel*: words aren't enough to express the emotions Jim feels, and Dean played these moments with a contorted, eloquent body language that was his hallmark as an actor. He was so alive on film in his brief career that he made as deep an impression as actors with many more years and many more films to their credit.

Fans will always think of James Dean in Rebel Without a Cause *whenever the subject of alienated youth comes up. Here he reacts in horror as he watches his friend, played by Sal Mineo, gunned down by the police.*

During their brief heyday in the 1930s, Jeanette MacDonald and Nelson Eddy were known to wags as "the Singing Capon taire and Rogers were united in dance.

In *Rose Marie,* MacDonald played a world-famous opera singer who treks through the Canadian wilderness to find her mous duet, the "Indian Love Call" (the song that goes, "When I'm calling you-hoo-oo-oo-oo-ooo-oo-oo...").

MacDonald was a lovely and funny actress who had begun her film career playing comical roles in light operettas such as *Love Me Tonight* (1932)

ABOVE: *The first film in the MacDonald–Eddy collaboration was the 1935 adaptation of Victor Herbert's operetta* Naughty Marietta, *in which she played a princess and he an Indian scout.*

Eddy and MacDonald were known to wags as "the Singing Capon and the Iron Butterfly" and to their fans as "America's Sweethearts." They are pictured here in New Moon *(1940), the seventh of the musicals they made together.*

and the Iron Butterfly." It is true that Eddy was not much of an actor and that the plots of their films together were sweetly sentimental, but to their legions of fans, they were "America's Sweethearts," united in song the way that As-outlaw brother (a very young James Stewart), while Eddy was the Mountie who is on his trail. They fall in love amid the fresh air of the pine forest, with the highlight of the film coming with their most fa-

>>>>>>>>>>>>

Rose Marie

(1936)

Screenplay by Frances Goodrich, Albert Hackett, and Alice Duer Miller, based on the musical by Otto A. Harbach and Oscar Hammerstein II. Songs by Otto Harbach, Oscar Hammerstein II, and Rudolf Friml; Gus Kahn and Herbert Stothart; Sam Lewis, Joe Young, and Harry Akst; Shelton Brooks. Produced by Hunt Stromberg. Directed by W. S. Van Dyke.

(MGM) 113 m.

<<<

Jeanette MacDonald was an opera singer trekking through the Canadian wilderness in search of her brother and Nelson Eddy was the Mountie who crosses her path in the operetta Rose Marie, *the second of the couple's ten popular films together.*

and *The Merry Widow* (1934), both of which found her paired with Maurice Chevalier. Her natural charms and screen presence offset Eddy's stiffness and lack of spontaneity. In *Rose Marie,* they represented a sort of idyllic sweetness as out of fashion today as the light operatic music they sang, he in his stentorian baritone, she in her cultured soprano. Still, a generation of filmgoers fondly recall the ten movies they made together, for, as MacDonald herself later said, "Sentiment, after all, is basic."

Jane Fonda has gone through many phases in her life and career: adorable ingenue, European sex kitten, militant antiwar activist, somewhat softer supporter of liberal causes, and now exercise queen. In the 1960s, her famous family name and her marriage to flashy European director Roger Vadim, as well as her generally undistinguished

Klute
(1971)
Screenplay by Andy K. Lewis and Dave Lewis. Produced and directed by Alan J. Pakula.
(Warner Bros.) 114 m.

choices of roles—*Barbarella* (1968), directed by her husband, being perhaps the most undistinguished—caused her to be taken less than seriously. But that changed with her breakthrough performance in the harrowing *They Shoot Horses, Don't They?* (1969). It was right in the midst of her radical days that she gave her most powerful performance as a classy Manhattan call girl stalked by a killer in *Klute*. Fonda intensely distrusted Hollywood at this stage of her career, but that didn't prevent her from doing some of her most precise work in this thriller.

Fonda thoroughly researched her role, spending hours with a Manhattan call girl and visiting bordellos (she reconciled her appearance in the film with her radical beliefs by publicly emphasizing the ex-

Fonda, in one of her ingenue, post-European sex queen roles, played newlywed Cory Bradder in Neil Simon's Barefoot in the Park *(1967). She is pictured here with co-star Robert Redford.*

Jane Fonda won her first Oscar for her sharply observed performance as New York call girl Bree Daniels, preyed upon by a psychopathic killer, in Klute.

ploitation of prostitutes in capitalist societies). Bree is a complex creature: protective of her privacy, relishing her control

veneer. And at this stage in her career, she still possessed a vulnerability and a lack of vanity that gave the role a risky feel. Her scenes with Sutherland, or the scenes in which Bree consults with her therapist that feature several lengthy monologues do not seem "acted" at all, but the utterances and behavior of a real person. Irony of ironies, "Hanoi Jane"—one of the most disliked actresses by the Hollywood establishment at the time—was so good in this film that she won that oft-touted popularity contest, the Oscar.

ABOVE: *Fonda won another in a long list of Oscar nominations for her role as a drunken, washed-up Hollywood actress who wakes up one morning to find a murdered man in her bed in* The Morning After *(1986).*

over men and their desires, and both enjoying and resenting her growing reliance on John Klute (Donald Sutherland), the detective who is trying to shield her from her pursuer. With almost surgical precision, Fonda suggested the emotional undertow beneath her character's surface control, the cracks in the Teflon

RIGHT: *Fonda was a major, highly respected star by 1977, when she took on the role of writer Lillian Hellman for the film* Julia, *based on some sections of Hellman's book* Pentimento.

105

✦ DIRTY HARRY ✦

During the first-run engagement of *Dirty Harry* in 1972, the rogue detective played by Clint Eastwood came to represent for many the celebrated law-and-order

When not playing Dirty Harry, Eastwood made two larkish comedies in which he appeared as a truck driver-cum-bare knuckles boxer with a baboon named Clyde for a pet. He is pictured here in the second film, Any Which Way You Can *(1980). The first was* Every Which Way But Loose *(1978).*

platform of then-president Richard Nixon. As a star, Eastwood appeared to be stepping into John Wayne's shoes, becoming the figurehead of love-it-or-leave-it Americanism. But just as Wayne and his characters

always had more depth than his detractors would admit, Eastwood and his incorruptible detective, Harry Callahan, were far from the wooden political symbols that they were taken to be.

By the time of *Dirty Harry* Eastwood was in charge of his career. He took the project through two studios before it was made at Warner Brothers with his choice of director, action specialist Don Siegel, with whom he had worked successfully on two previous occasions. The film clearly meant a great deal to Eastwood. He even directed some sequences when Siegel was ill. With his pompadour and V-neck sweater, Harry looked square for his time, but his stoic inscrutability was decidedly hip. As he tracks a

Dirty Harry
(1971)
Screenplay by Harry Julian Fink, Rita M. Fink, and Dean Riesner. Produced and directed by Don Siegel.
(Warner Bros.) 103 m.

mad sniper (Andy Robinson) through San Francisco, his biggest beef is not with his prey but with a media-conscious City Hall that will not let him do his job. Curiously, he is a rebel and

After a stint in TV's Rawhide, *Eastwood achieved international stardom playing the Man with No Name in three Sergio Leone "spaghetti" Westerns, the second of which,* For a Few Dollars More *(1965), is pictured here.*

This celebrated early scene in Dirty Harry *set the stage for the entire series, as the San Francisco detective played by Clint Eastwood foils a robbery during his lunch break and bluffs the "punk" at left into surrendering his weapon, all the while chewing on a bite of a hot dog.*

an authority figure at the same time. For every tag line or favorite scene—Harry calmly munching on a hot dog as he hinders a midday crime, climaxed by the immortal "Do you feel lucky, punk?" soliloquy—there is a moment in which the actor effectively conveys the painful frustration un-

derlying Callahan's manhunt (which would steadily diminish with each sequel).

Steely eyed and enigmatic, Eastwood is perhaps the last in a long line of American screen actors, like Wayne, Gary Cooper, and Spencer Tracy, who excelled at portraying men of action rather than thought. For

men like these, emotions remain unspoken, divined through deed. But when Harry throws his badge in the dirty water at the end of the film, he expresses his pain eloquently enough.

⫷ LOVE FINDS ANDY HARDY ⫸

"**G**osh dad, a fellow can't take two girls to the same dance!" says Andy in *Love Finds Andy Hardy*. Such are the concerns of the so-called typical American teenager circa 1938. And such is the central plot point of the fourth and most famous of

cious talent with energy to burn.

The series was low-budget, and depended quite a bit on Rooney's powerhouse characterization for its entertainment value. Andy Hardy may not have been wholly representative of America's youth—it is doubtful that any

```
>>>>>>>>>>>>>>
```

Love Finds Andy Hardy
(1938)
Screenplay by William Ludwig, based on stories by Vivien R. Bretherton, from characters created by Aurania Rouverol. Directed by George B. Seitz.
(MGM) 90 m.

As Andy Hardy, the prototypical teenager of the 1930s and 1940s, Mickey Rooney offered millions of moviegoers a comforting image of American youth, as in Love Finds Andy Hardy, *pictured here. He co-starred with Judy Garland in several of the series' offerings.*

the 16-film MGM series. At the center, of course, was Mickey Rooney's Andy. Rooney, an MGM star since childhood, was a preco-

teenager was ever so entirely innocent—but he was a popular figure because he offered moviegoers such a comforting image of

the younger generation: decent, clean-cut, worried about nothing more than getting a date for the Christmas dance, and adoring of his wise old father (Lewis Stone).

Rooney was all over the place in this movie and in nearly every scene, wooing girls (including a young Lana Turner), wise-acring his sister (Cecilia Parker), trying to figure out how to buy a used car without his father knowing about it, comforting his mother (Fay Holden). Rooney and his fellow MGM juveniles were under great pressure at the studio—he made no fewer than four Andy Hardy films in 1938, in addition to *Boy's Town*—and his manic, nonstop invention in the role may reflect the desperation of a young actor trying to keep up. In *Love Finds Andy Hardy*, at least he was assisted by Judy Garland, charming as Betsy, the girl next door who falls for everyone's favorite boy.

Lawrence of Arabia, director David Lean's version of the life of British adventurer and author T. E. Lawrence, may seem at times like the "biggest movie ever made." The sheer bulk of the spectacle on screen, filmed against one spectacular Super Panavision desert expanse after another, gives the epic an immense scale. It took a great, dynamic performance to keep the drama of Lawrence from choking on so much desert sand, and that is exactly what Peter O'Toole delivered.

O'Toole had garnered only a few supporting parts in films when he won the role of the World War I colonel who led the Arab revolt against the Ottoman Empire, beating such contenders as Marlon Brando, Alec Guinness, and Anthony Perkins. Whether that made him lucky or not became a debatable point, at least at the time, for filming under the hot desert sun was so trying that it was years before the actor could even watch the result. Lawrence, as conceived by Lean

Two years after making his first screen appearance, Peter O'Toole soared to stardom as T. E. Lawrence, the British adventurer who leads an Arab army into battle in Lawrence of Arabia.

Lawrence of Arabia
(1962)
Screenplay by Robert Bolt.
Produced by Sam Spiegel.
Directed by David Lean.
(Columbia) 221 m.

and his writer Robert Bolt, was a contradictory fellow—charming, relentless, beloved by the Arab factions he tried to unite but also a merciless imperialist and a megalomaniac. O'Toole caught all of these qualities in his performance, particularly the mania of power. Perhaps the most telling moment came early on when Lawrence casually puts out a match with his fingers. When asked what was the trick, he replies blithely, "The trick is not minding the pain." Most interesting of all, however, was the suggestion of sexual ambiguity in Lawrence, brought to life by O'Toole's effeminate walk and the odd overtones of masochism in the scene in which he is whipped by a Turkish bey (José Ferrer). This plum came to O'Toole very early on in his long career, and although he has scored numerous other triumphs, his first starring role may prove to be his grandest.

❧ FATAL ATTRACTION ❧

Many of Hollywood's leading actresses read for

After Fatal Attraction, *Close was offered more dastardly roles. Here she is the evil Marquise de Merteuil, plotting an elaborate seduction of an innocent with the incorrigible libertine Valmont (John Malkovich) in the 1988 adaptation of Choderos de Laclos'* Dangerous Liaisons.

the role of Alex Forrest, a suicidal obsessive who won't let a married man (Michael Douglas) walk away from a weekend fling, and many turned it down. The one who said "yes" was Glenn Close, who until then had ordinarily been cast as mother figures in films such as

The World According to Garp (1982) and *The Big Chill* (1983). For her, a steady actress who had never exhibited much sex appeal, Alex offered a genuine opportunity. And she made the most of it, bringing an electrifying charge to the screen.

Her hair teased into golden, Medusa-like ringlets, her plain-Jane features enhanced by a perpetual, desperate smile, Close's Alex is an initially charming, witty, and vivacious career woman, whose first meeting with Douglas' Dan Gallagher is deceptively unassuming: as they speak, she zeroes in on him like a

predator. Close conveyed, with pinpoint accuracy and an intensity that never let up, the wildness of Alex's mood swings—her frenzied lust, her suicide attempt, her cloying attention to Dan that turns pathological. The most chilling scene in the film might be that in which Dan comes home to find Alex amiably chatting with his wife (Anne Archer). One doesn't

Glenn Close had specialized in motherly characters before she turned the tables as the suicidal obsessive Alex Forrest in Fatal Attraction.

Here the initially charming, witty, and vivacious Alex seduces businessman Dan Gallagher (Michael Douglas) in Fatal Attraction.

know what Alex will do from one moment to the next.

Fatal Attraction originally ended with Alex committing suicide after planting evidence to convict Dan of murder. When preview audiences found it depressing, it was replaced by the current ending, in which Alex becomes a lethal monster straight out of a horror film. It is a tribute to Close's acting that both possibilities seem viable.

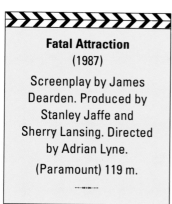

Fatal Attraction
(1987)
Screenplay by James Dearden. Produced by Stanley Jaffe and Sherry Lansing. Directed by Adrian Lyne.
(Paramount) 119 m.

By the early 1940s, Joan Crawford seemed washed-up in movies. The devil-may-care flapper roles she made famous were no longer in vogue, and she was aging. After she was politely released from her MGM contract by studio chief Louis B. Mayer, she signed on at Warner Brothers—with a salary cut. She knew that she needed a role that would restore her career. She even took herself off the studio payroll for a time because she didn't read any scripts that she liked. Then she read *Mildred Pierce*.

Crawford was perfect as the hard-as-nails waitress who works her way up to a world of

affluence in order to give her spoiled daughter, Veda (Ann Blyth) a better life. Crawford reinvented herself for the part: the coiffed, elegantly made-up MGM siren gave way to a less polished, tawdrier looking woman. Appropriately, she effected this transformation at a more cost-conscious studio, one that prided itself on its depictions of working-class America.

ABOVE: *Joan Crawford, during the early flapper state of her long career, is the life of the party in the 1928 silent film* Our Dancing Daughters.

LEFT: *Between her early flapper roles during the silent era and the more realistic characters she portrayed in the 1940s, Crawford appeared in a series of lush, glamorous films at MGM during the 1930s. One of the most famous of these was* Grand Hotel (1932), *in which she played a typist for a businessman played by Wallace Beery.*

>>>>>>>>>>>>>>>>>

Mildred Pierce
(1945)
Screenplay by Ranald
MacDougall and Catherine
Turney, based on the novel
by James M. Cain.
Produced by Jerry Wald.
Directed by Michael Curtiz.
(Warner Bros.) 113 m.

Ultimately, Crawford's determination to prove herself was the equal of Mildred's drive to give Veda everything she wants. The actress won an Oscar for *Mildred Pierce*. Small wonder: the hard, icy precision for which she became noted in the second half of her career was born here, and it would never seem more appropriate, nor so vital.

After being let go by MGM, Joan Crawford made her comeback at Warner Brothers, where she won an Oscar as a mother who will do anything for her daughter in the hard-boiled film Mildred Pierce.

MARTY

Marty, writer Paddy Chayefsky's lovely story of two homely nobodies from the Bronx who find love together, was originally created for television with Rod Steiger in the title role. Steiger's interpretation accentuated the drabness of the character as well as his intensity. Ernest Borgnine won an Oscar and permanent stardom with his eminently lovable, poignant portrayal for the film version.

Borgnine's most affecting characteristic is his big, heartwarming, unaffected grin. In film after film, he played unintelligent characters, babies at heart in a bear-like body who smile through every mood. His Fatso in *From Here to Eternity* (1953), for instance, grins through his most sadistic moments. In *Marty,* the smile was a heartbreaking cover for the loneliness of the good-hearted Bronx butcher who lives with his mother and spends every Saturday night with his equally lonely pals. The well-known rhythmic cadences of Chayefsky's dialogue—"Whadda you wanna do tonight, Marty?" "I don't know, whadda you wanna do tonight, Ange?"—may seem more formulaic

Marty
(1955)
Story and screenplay by Paddy Chayefsky. Produced by Harold Hecht. Directed by Delbert Mann.
(United Artists) 91 m.

now than they once did, but Marty's romance with Clara (Betsy Blair), the ugly duckling he meets at a dance hall and falls for against the advice of his friends and mother, remains moving. As Borgnine played it, Marty is a sort of realistic male Cinderella, who pulls himself out of his aimless rut by his own initiative. It is a magical moment when Marty finally listens to his own heart and calls Clara on the phone. Borgnine, with that trademark eagerness, his rough-hewn Italian-American voice, and of course the ear-to-ear grin, played that climactic scene as if his heart were about to burst with joy.

Ernest Borgnine won an Oscar for his performance as the Bronx butcher who falls in love for the first time with a kind but plain school teacher (Betsy Blair) in Marty.

❦ BULLITT ❦

Perhaps of all the action stars of the movies, Steve McQueen was the most laconic, the most tight-lipped, the most enigmatic. If his popularity seems somewhat inexplicable now, it is important to remember that in his heyday McQueen bridged a significant gap in American culture between the no-nonsense tough guys of the 1930s and 1940s and the antiheroes of the 1960s and 1970s. Perhaps more than anything else it was his nearly mystical comfort with silence—he probably had fewer lines of dialogue in his career than any star in Hollywood since the advent of the talkies—and his faint air of disdain for authority that made him popular with the nation's alienated youth.

These qualities are exemplified in *Bullitt,* the first film

Bullitt
(1968)
Screenplay by Harry Kleiner and Alan R. Trustman, based on the novel Mute Witness by Robert L. Pike. Produced by Philip D'Antoni. Directed by Peter Yates.
(Warner Bros.) 113 m.

---

made by McQueen's production company, Solar. His police detective is not disrespectful of authority, as Gene Hackman's Popeye Doyle or Clint Eastwood's Dirty Harry Callahan would be just three years later, nor is he a tough loner—he has a happy, if quiet, relationship with his girlfriend (Jacqueline Bisset). But he distrusts the local, media-hungry politician (Robert Vaughn) who puts him and his men in danger in order to protect a mob witness. Also, the black turtleneck that McQueen wore in the role marked him as a decidedly hip figure amongst the "establishment" politicians. It doesn't seem like much today but in 1968, jacket, tie, and porkpie hat seemed to be regulation for movie cops, such as Richard Widmark in *Madigan,* made the same year as *Bullitt.*

McQueen was at his most convincing, however, behind the wheel of a car. *Bullitt* really revs

With his black turtleneck and disdain for a suave politician played by Robert Vaughn, Steve McQueen's San Francisco cop in Bullitt started Hollywood down the road toward a host of anti-hero police films. McQueen also produced the movie and executed many of his own auto stunts.

up during its justifiably famous high-speed chase sequence through the streets and outskirts of San Francisco. The emphasis on action at the expense of plot or character development, a novelty in its time but par for the course now, paid off. McQueen, a racing enthusiast in real life, was certainly built for speed as a star.

TERMS OF ENDEARMENT

Like the situation between their characters, Shirley MacLaine and Debra Winger, who played mother and daughter in *Terms of Endearment,* were very much at odds throughout the filming. Indeed, the generational conflict frequently exploded into tense verbal exchanges. For all the pain of getting there, however, the result was one of the most popular films of the 1980s and an Oscar for MacLaine as Best Actress.

The stubborn, queenly Aurora Greenaway, a wealthy widow who tells a moving man, "Be careful with that

Shirley MacLaine won an Oscar for her performance as Aurora Greenaway, a tyrannically adoring mother who learns to loosen up over the years, in Terms of Endearment.

Terms of Endearment
(1983)
Screenplay by James L.
Brooks, based on the novel
by Larry McMurtry.
Produced and directed by
James L. Brooks.
(Paramount) 132 m.

painting—it's worth more money than you'll make in your entire life," was a terrific showcase for the mature actress. In it, she was able to retain some of the pertness and girlishness that made her a star in the 1950s, while at the same time gamely exploring the lonely middle age of her charac-ter. Her scenes with Jack Nicholson, as the next-door neighbor and former astronaut, are the film's funniest and most poignant, with Aurora both attracted to and re-pelled by this handsome, crude fellow. The film's second half, however, has a scene that is probably the most forceful of MacLaine's entire career. In it, Aurora keeps watch as Winger's Emma lies in a hospi-tal bed dying of cancer. When she sees that her daughter is suffering, she goes to a nurse to ask for her daughter's pain-relieving medication. The at-

In Vincente Minnelli's Some Came Running *(1959), Mac-Laine played one of the pert, girlish roles that characterized the early part of her career.*

tendant's indifference and her motherly attachments force her into an emotional explosion that turns the hospital upside down.

When MacLaine won the Oscar, she said, "I really de-serve this," perhaps a reference to the travails of making the film. Still, when one recalls that perfectly calibrated, ex-plosive hospital scene, it's hard not to agree.

MacLaine demonstrated her ample talents as a dancer in Sweet Charity, *the 1969 film adaptation of the Neil Simon–Cy Cole-man–Dorothy Fields musical based on Fed-erico Fellini's film* Nights of Cabiria *(1957).*

A SHOT IN THE DARK

Peter Sellers' first movie as the bumbling Inspector Clouseau was The *Pink Panther* (1964), but the character, for which Peter Ustinov was the original choice, was subsidiary to David Niven's cat burglar, Sir Charles Lytton. It became apparent very early on that Sellers was, pardon the pun, stealing the movie, so, knowing he had a good thing, Blake Edwards went into production with *A Shot in the Dark,* the first full-fledged Inspector Clouseau vehicle, almost immediately after the first film wrapped.

"Where do you think you're going?" asks a man of Inspector Clouseau before he walks fully dressed into a nudist colony. "I don't think! I know where I'm going," he answers, when, of course, he hasn't the slightest idea. It was arrogance such as this, totally unsupported by Clouseau's aptitudes, that made the character so delightful. In *A Shot in the Dark,* Clouseau, bumbling and stumbling his way toward solving a murder mystery, is motivated by his valiant love for the chief suspect (Elke Sommer). Along the way he becomes the bane of the existence of Chief Inspector Dreyfus (Herbert Lom), who muses: "Give me ten men like Clouseau and I could destroy the world."

Sellers was an expert at physical comedy, but the extra, brilliant touch he brought to the role was that of a man who sees himself as totally in control, always dignified, an idea that Sellers drew from a matchbook cover that showed a prototypically stiff-upper-lipped Englishman. Clouseau's pratfalls are hilarious, but his attempts at

LEFT: *Clouseau is here engaged in one of his insane, impromptu karate practices with his butler Kato in* The Pink Panther Strikes Again *(1976), the fourth Pink Panther movie.*

RIGHT: *Clouseau pretends to be a mountain climber in order to sneak into the castle of Inspector Dreyfus (Herbert Lom), who was driven so mad by Clouseau that he has become an evil genius bent on destroying the world, in* The Pink Panther Strikes Again.

⫸⫸⫸⫸⫸⫸⫸⫸⫸

A Shot in the Dark
(1964)
Screenplay by Blake
Edwards and William Peter
Blatty, based on plays by
Harry Kurnitz and Marcel
Achard. Produced and
directed by Blake Edwards
(United Artists) 101 m.

⸺⸻⸺

*Clouseau in one of his many dis-
guises, here as a Swedish fisher-
man, in Sellers' final appearance
in the Pink Panther series,* The
Revenge of the Pink Panther
(1978). *After the actor's death in
1980, director Blake Edwards
tried to keep the series going
with two more films starring
Ted Wass as Clouseau's nephew,
the first of which featured out-
takes of Sellers from past Pink
Panther outings.*

pretending that nothing
has happened are the
icing on the cake. For
example, a simple re-
quest from George
Sanders' Monsieur
Ballon to put away a
pool cue results in the
total destruction of every
cue on the rack, each at-
tempt to cover up the *faux pas*

resulting in more embarrassment, with Ballon watching in a
perfect George Sanders deadpan.
Sellers also devised a French accent in which every word spoken
was a comic event. The actor
starred in three more Pink Panther films before his death in
1980. It is in the 1975 *The Return of the Pink Panther* that
Clouseau mispronounces the
word "monkey" as "minkeh."

*Peter Sellers based his portrayal
of the bumbling In-
spector Clouseau
on a match-
book cover
that showed a
prototypically
stiff-upper-
lipped En-
glishman.
Every word
he spoke in
his hilarious
French accent was
a comic event.*

There was a fragile quality about Montgomery Clift—it seemed at times that he might break. Beneath his matinee-idol good looks (ruined later in his life by a disfiguring auto accident as well as years of drug and alcohol abuse) one sensed a residue of deep pain. He was not a showy actor, but a quiet, concentrated one.

From Here to Eternity
(1953)
Screenplay by Daniel Taradash, from the novel by James Jones. Produced by Buddy Adler. Directed by Fred Zinnemann.
(Columbia) 118 m.

Some might have said that he lacked a reliable instrument—he could be physically awkward and his voice tended to quaver. But it didn't matter. He worked from stillness, and few could match his brooding intensity.

Columbia Pictures wanted a tougher actor, like Aldo Ray or John Derek, to play the role of a career soldier in pre–World War II Hawaii, who is given "the treat-ment" by the officers and non-coms of his unit for refusing to box, having once blinded a man in the ring. But James Jones, the author of the novel, insisted on Clift (probably the one thing that Jones liked about the film). To ready himself for the part, the actor went into training and learned to play the bugle, at which Prewitt excels. Ironically, perhaps it was awkwardness that made his portrayal so special. Here he was, playing a military man and a boxer but, unlike most actors, he didn't emphasize the character's tough-ness (he couldn't learn to fight convincingly, a problem that also plagued him on the 1948 Western, *Red River*). He focused instead on Prewitt's sensitivity, movingly evidenced in the scene in which he explains why he won't box anymore. It was a performance of typically quiet intensity, and what the viewer remembers is the steadfastness, the courage, the loyalty, and the love that Prewitt has for his dancehall girlfriend, Lorene (Donna Reed), and his army pal, the unlucky Maggio (Frank Sinatra). Clift's crowning moment as an actor might have been the scene in which his char-acter stands alone in the dark-ness playing a mournful taps for

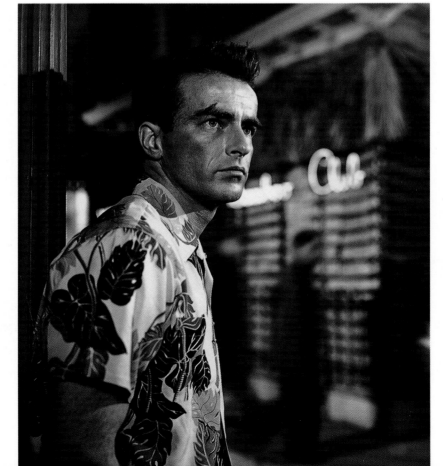

his unfortunate friend. There was no playact-ing here—he let the scene and the moment speak for themselves.

In From Here to Eternity, *Mont-gomery Clift deliv-ered a performance of typically quiet in-tensity, playing an army career man who is harassed by the officers and non-coms of his company for refusing to box.*

Dudley Moore made his name in the 1960s as part of the four-man British revue, Beyond the Fringe (comedian-actor Peter Cook, playwright Alan Bennett, and writer-director Jonathan Miller were the others). His film career didn't take off, however, until his supporting role as a mad conductor in the 1978 film *Foul Play,* followed by his 1979 starring role in Blake Edwards' *10.* Two years later he made his definitive screen appearance in *Arthur.*

Moore had always been good at drunk scenes, and, recognizing this, writer-director Steve Gordon (who died at a young age not too long after *Arthur,* his directorial debut, was released)

Arthur
(1981)
Screenplay by Steve Gordon. Produced by Robert Greenhut. Directed by Steve Gordon.
(Orion) 97 m.

---

fashioned many giddy, drunken moments for him to chew on. Arthur is a carefree millionaire who happily, irresponsibly, drinks his life away, with all of

his needs met by his faithful valet, Hobson (John Gielgud). Like a child, enjoying toy trains and wearing cowboy hats, Arthur experiences mature

love and sober reality for the first time when he meets a down-to-earth woman named Linda Marola (Liza Minnelli) who has little interest in his millions.

What Moore brought to the role was a bumbling glee, and an angelic, scatterbrained sloppiness. Although the relationship between Arthur and Linda is engaging, perhaps the best scenes in the film are those between the millionaire and his butler. Moore's casual, slurred

line readings were offered fine comic contrast by Gielgud's clipped, sardonic, deadpan reserve. When, for example,

Cuddly, rich, and perhaps the most vivacious drunk in New York, Arthur Bach, the title character in Arthur, *captivated moviegoers everywhere, setting Dudley Moore, who played him, on the road to a series of not nearly as successful romantic comedies.*

Arthur asks Hobson to draw his bath, the butler replies, "It is what I live for" and then promptly sits down to read his newspaper. Moore was executive producer of the 1988 sequel, *Arthur 2: on the Rocks.*

Today *Casablanca* is considered the quintessential Hollywood film, but when it went into production it was just another Warner Brothers project, originally slated to star Ann Sheridan and Ronald Reagan. No doubt movie lovers everywhere thank the fates for putting Ingrid Bergman and Humphrey Bogart in their places.

The swirling intrigue of the action centers around Rick's American Bar in Casablanca, a watering hole frequented by European refugees en route to America during World War II. The atmospheric sets and the cynical byplay of a score of brilliant character actors provide the backdrop for the reunion of Bogart's Rick and Bergman's Ilsa, lovers in Paris be-

fore the war who were torn apart by an odd turn of events. Through a twist of fate, they meet again in Casablanca, where they must sacrifice their love once more for the Allied cause. As a couple, they are seen only in a few brief scenes. The most memorable moments are those in which they are apart, remembering their love affair. Bergman was photographed lov-

ingly, her face glowing with romance, and though her part was actually relatively minor compared to many of those she would play throughout her career, she will always be remembered for those tearstained close-ups that moved audiences everywhere. As for Bogart, who can ever forget that famous moment when Rick walks into the bar to stop Dooley Wilson's Sam from playing "As Time Goes By"? When Rick sees Ilsa by the piano, there is a close-up of Bogart in which his face seems to turn to stone, and in that instant every jilted lover sees the embodiment of that horrible feeling he or she has known. Later, as Rick sits at a table and stares bitterly into the distance, he utters the immortal lines: "Of all the gin joints in all the world, she walks into mine," and again every heart watching him aches. Bogart and Bergman in *Casablanca* are the soul of Hollywood.

OPPOSITE: *One of the most memorable scenes in Hollywood history came at the end of* Casablanca, *when Rick Blaine (Humphrey Bogart) puts Ilsa Lund (Ingrid Bergman) on a plane to safety and forgoes their life together, saying "The problems of two people don't amount to a hill of beans in this crazy world."*

In flashback, audiences see the flowering of the affair between Ilsa and Rick, who have found themselves reunited in the turmoil of refugee-haunted Casablanca during World War II. Here, as part of the flashback, Ilsa and Rick watch the Germans march into Paris, bringing their romantic idyll to an end.

Casablanca
(1943)
Produced by Hal B. Wallis. Screenplay by Julius J. and Phillip G. Epstein and Howard Koch, based on the play *Everybody Comes To Rick's* by Murray Burnett and Joan Alison. Directed by Michael Curtiz.
(Warner Bros.) 102 m.

TAXI DRIVER

Taxi Driver is the film that put Robert De Niro on the map as the major actor of his generation. Although he had distinguished himself in a number of stellar roles before the 1976 film and had even won an Oscar as the young Don Corleone in *The Godfather, Part II* (1974), it was the almost uncomfortably intimate level on which he met Travis Bickle that marked him as an actor of acute concentration and frightening intuition and perception. Jeff Bridges almost played the role, and while he would undoubtedly have done well with it, it is difficult to imagine that he could have come within hailing distance of De Niro's astonishing work.

Travis, as written by Paul Schrader, is an extremely complex character, at once perceptive and, at the same time, inarticulate and awkward around people. He is a lonely midwestern Vietnam vet transplanted to New York, who dreams of being somebody. He also has an acute case of paranoia that blossoms into multiple murders, and his own ambiguities are perplexing. For example, at one moment he is sitting in an all-night porno house, and later he rails against "the scum, the dogs, the filth" of New York's

De Niro gave a moving performance as a man who has been revived after a 30-year bout with a rare sleeping sickness in Awakenings *(1990).*

As Travis Bickle, a lonely midwestern Vietnam vet transplanted to New York in Taxi Driver, *Robert De Niro delivered a performance of startling intensity and intimacy. It was his work on this film that established him as the major actor of his generation.*

mean streets in his diary. De Niro, in collaboration with his director Martin Scorsese, burrowed into the role and found a disturbing way of moving

and speaking for his character that is almost frighteningly intense: it is as though Travis has built a little world for himself alone.

In a performance rich in memorable moments, perhaps the most telling are those in which Travis fumbles his way through a date with Cybill Shepherd's Betsy and those in which he practices drawing his gun in front of the mirror in his apartment, uttering his famous line, "You talkin' to me?" which the actor improvised. The chilling consequences of his behavior come in the apocalyptic ending,

De Niro won his first Oscar as the youthful Don Corleone in The Godfather, Part II *(1974).*

De Niro won his second Oscar for his galvanic performance as middleweight fighter Jake La Motta in Raging Bull *(1980). The actor's acute concentration and frightening intuition continued to flower in this film, a high point in his ongoing collaboration with director Martin Scorsese.*

in which Travis guns down every inhabitant of a Lower East Side whorehouse to "save" the 13-year-old Iris (Jodie Foster).

Taxi Driver
(1976)
Screenplay by Paul Schrader. Produced by Michael and Julia Philips. Directed by Martin Scorsese.
(Columbia) 114 m.

THE PHILADELPHIA STORY

In 1939, Katharine Hepburn's career in movies was at its nadir. Her New England sophistication and tremulous ingenue act had become box-office poison. In an effort to save her career, she went to New York and scored a triumph in the stage play *The Philadelphia Story*, written specifically for her by Philip Barry. In it, she played Tracy Lord, a haughty young society woman who learns to be a better person on the eve of her wedding to a caustic social climber.

The Philadelphia Story
(1940)
Screenplay by Donald Ogden Stewart, based on the play by Philip Barry. Produced by Joseph L. Mankiewicz. Directed by George Cukor.
(MGM) 112 m.

Badly needing a movie hit, Hepburn went to MGM to recreate her Broadway success. Given considerable control over the lavish production, she judiciously surrounded herself with talent on both sides of the camera (she wanted Clark Gable and Spencer Tracy for the male leads, but had to settle for Cary Grant and James Stewart!). The effort paid off, and *The Philadelphia Story* single-handedly restored her popularity with movie-goers.

Was it any accident that the heroine, Tracy Lord, was comically upbraided by the men in her life and reduced through the action of the play from an icy "queen" to a "human being"? Hepburn herself was perceived as hoity-toity by the public, and the film made her seem more lifesize, as it heightened her glamour. For in the course of humanizing Tracy, *Philadelphia Story* serves up a number of moments in which the character is taught cruel lessons about humanity by her father (John Halliday) and ex-husband (Grant). In these instances Hepburn made the pain palpable. There are also moments when her gorgeous, perfectly angled face, fuller than in her 1930s roles, lights up the screen. When, for example, Grant's C. K. Dexter Haven leans up close to her as she sleeps, her face glowing with beauty, and whispers, "You look beautiful, Red," he seems to be right on the money.

LEFT: *Katharine Hepburn won her second of four Oscars—a record for a performer—in 1968, as Eleanor of Aquitane in the medieval drama* The Lion in Winter.

OPPOSITE: *After being labeled "box-office poison," Katharine Hepburn went to New York and scored a triumph in the stage play* The Philadelphia Story, *written specifically for her by Philip Barry. She came back to Hollywood and re-created her stage role, that of haughty heiress Tracy Lord, in the film, which co-starred Cary Grant as her ex-husband.*

LA DOLCE VITA

For the lead of his ornate pageant of decadence, *La Dolce Vita,* director Federico Fellini sought out someone with an ordinary face whom no one would remember. He chose Marcello Mastroianni, a hardworking actor who had not yet made much of an impression in Italian films. Although women everywhere might disagree with Fellini's assessment of Mastroianni's looks, there is an ordinariness about him. He comes across as a regular guy who just happens to possess chic, grace and a self-deprecating wit. This mix was perfect for his namesake role, as a reporter leading the Roman "sweet life" of the title.

Fellini did not send Mastroianni a script to engage him for *La Dolce Vita;* he proffered instead a dirty cartoon. And indeed today, the once controversial movie plays something like an animated short that could have been called "The Adventures of Marcello." The reporter romps with an American starlet (Anita Ekberg), ditches his fiancée for an alluring, pleasure-seeking woman (Anouk Aimee), witnesses a miracle that escalates into a media event with swarms of paparazzi, and finally presides over a grotesque orgy. Throughout all of this, Mastroianni's Marcello is sweetly bored and unflappable, thoughtfully discontented with his life, but a step away from sinking into a mire of mindless hedonism.

In the wake of *La Dolce Vita,* playing the disenchanted spectator was the actor's specialty—he brought to the screen the popular image of the world-weary charmer and became for many Americans the prototypical European male.

In La Dolce Vita, *Marcello Mastroianni played Marcello, a wayward Italian reporter pursuing an American film star (Anita Ekberg). Through his portrayal of this world-weary charmer, the then largely unknown actor became for many Americans the prototype of the European male.*

La Dolce Vita
(1960)
Screenplay by Federico Fellini, Tullio Pinelli, Ennio Flaiano and Brunello Rondi. Produced by Giuseppe Amato. Directed by Federico Fellini.
(Riama) 173 m.

P S Y C H O

To say that Anthony Perkins played Norman Bates to perfection in Alfred Hitchcock's masterpiece seems an understatement. As one watches the film, his identification with the role seems so strong, so utterly complete, that the dividing line between Perkins and Bates becomes thin indeed. The boyish actor certainly felt a kinship with the ultimate "mama's boy," as he has attested in interviews, and has returned to play him in three sequels, the second (and best) of which he also directed. He has even hinted at the role to humorous effect in a 1990s cereal commercial for TV.

Perkins was Hitchcock's first and only choice for the role. He had already played gawky, ungainly young men in several films throughout the 1950s, and his schizophrenic baseball pitcher in *Fear Strikes Out* (1957) might now be seen as a dry run for *Psycho*. But when he played Norman, the kindly motel owner who has not quite "accepted" his mother's death, the all-American awkwardness became truly horrifying because of what lay beneath it. Hitchcock might have cast a score of plug-

As Norman Bates, Anthony Perkins recoils in shock from his "mother's" handiwork in Alfred Hitchcock's Psycho. *After a long hiatus from the role, Perkins returned to play Norman in three sequels, one of which he also directed.*

ugly character actors as his psycho (the character was based on real-life serial killer Ed Gein), but he deliberately chose someone disarming, someone who would not have been out of place on *Dobie Gillis*.

On repeated viewings, the details of Perkins' performance become increasingly fascinating: the feminine swagger as he runs to and from the house; the desperate politeness; the nervous vocal tics; the hawk-like way he watches people who might be threatening to his "mother," uncannily echoing the stuffed birds on Bates' wall; the compulsive eating of candy (the actor's own idea).

At the time the role was offered to him, Perkins was advised by friends to turn it down. But he thought that it

would make his career, and he was right. Perhaps his friends were right too. He was so good that every other role he has taken has seemed haunted by Norman Bates.

Psycho
(1960)
Screenplay by Joseph Stefano, from a novel by Robert Bloch. Produced and directed by Alfred Hitchcock.
(Paramount) 109 m.

Initially Paul Newman wanted to play Sundance, the taciturn straight man, in *Butch Cassidy and the Sundance Kid*. He felt that he would be unable to handle the comedy required of the verbose Butch, the "thinker" of the Hole in the Wall Gang. Finally the filmmakers convinced him otherwise. As for Sundance, Steve McQueen was the first choice, but he was unable to commit to the project, so Robert Redford, a young actor with a few striking performances to his credit, got the part.

This prototypical "buddy" movie, a comic look at the last days of the legendary Western bankrobbers as they flee from a super posse, was made in a spirit of real harmony by all concerned. It shows on the screen. Butch and Sundance may bicker like Ralph and Alice Kramden on *The Honeymooners*, but at the end of each disagreement they still have great affection for one another. (By contrast, Katharine Ross' Etta, Sundance's girlfriend who also loves Butch, seems merely decorative.)

Newman was the picture of cocky self-assurance and real *joie de vivre* as Butch, the one who sensibly decides that he and Sundance should take the famous precipitous dive into the water to evade their pur-

---

Butch Cassidy and the Sundance Kid
(1969)
Screenplay by William Goldman. Produced by John Foreman. Directed by George Roy Hill.
(20th Century Fox) 110 m.

---

suers, even though the Kid can't swim ("Are you crazy," he says, "the fall alone will probably kill you.") It is also his idea that they escape to Bolivia ("I guess this isn't the main part of the city," he says as he, Sundance, and Etta step off the train into a godforsaken landscape. "This might be the garden spot of the whole country," answers an infuriated Sundance. "People may travel hundreds of miles just to get to this spot where we're standing now.").

Butch's only blind spot, a discomfort over the use of violence, is made up for by Sundance's abundant confidence with firearms. Even though the Kid says precious little about the inevitability of their deaths, Redford brought to the part a dry fatalism that gave the movie its serious edge. Still, at the film's end, when the outlaws are holed up in a room in Bolivia, mortally wounded and surrounded by a large portion of the Bolivian army, Butch and Sundance continue to bicker. To them, it's the stuff of life.

Four years after Butch Cassidy and the Sundance Kid, *Newman (left) and Redford teamed again in* The Sting. *This time they played two Depression-era grifters out to play "the big con" on a gangster (Robert Shaw).*

THE SUNDANCE KID

Audiences in the rebellious 1960s were taken with the lighthearted revisionist Western Butch Cassidy and the Sundance Kid, *in which Paul Newman played the cocky outlaw Butch Cassidy and Robert Redford the sullen, fast-drawing Sundance Kid. Here the end of the film finds them prepared to defend themselves against much of the Bolivian army.*

Garbo. The name still conjures up mystery, longing, and loneliness. With her brooding eyes, swan-like body, and slow, rhythmic way of moving, she seemed to have a magnetic pull that made her different from other movie stars. An aura of fate seemed to loom over Garbo onscreen, coupled with the sense of deep passion that she was able to summon as an actress. She made magic in each film of her brief career.

She was at her peak when she appeared in the role she

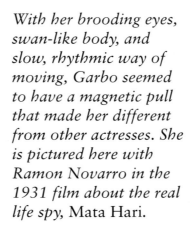

With her brooding eyes, swan-like body, and slow, rhythmic way of moving, Garbo seemed to have a magnetic pull that made her different from other actresses. She is pictured here with Ramon Novarro in the 1931 film about the real life spy, Mata Hari.

was "born to play," as her director, George Cukor, put it, the 19th-century Parisian prostitute in *Camille*, based on Alexandre Dumas' immortal love story. She had excelled at showing the intoxication of love in the past: consider her slow walk as she "memorizes" the room where she has fallen in love in *Queen Christina* (1933). Her special

qualities made her perfect for Marguerite, the courtesan whose love for Armand (Robert Taylor), a young man above her lowly station, flow-

LEFT: *Garbo is seen here in the famous final moments of* Queen Christina *(1933), in which she played the Scandinavian monarch who abdicated the throne for love. Her director, Rouben Mamoulian, told her not to think of anything—he simply wanted her to stare blankly ahead, all the better to concentrate on her mysterious, lonely face.*

In Camille, *the crowning role of her career, Greta Garbo played Marguerite Gautier, the 19th-century Parisian courtesan who is in love with nobleman Armand (Robert Taylor).*

LEFT: *Garbo, pictured here with her favorite leading man, John Gilbert, was adept at showing the intoxication of love, amply demonstrated in this scene from* Flesh and the Devil *(1926).*

ers as she fades away from tuberculosis. It is difficult to imagine any other actress handling with such grace and delicacy the legendary death scene in which Marguerite valiantly tries to hide her condition from her lover. Irving Thalberg, MGM's talented young production chief and the man who oversaw Garbo's career after her arrival in Hollywood from Sweden in 1925, died early in the making of the film, which may have inspired Garbo and all concerned to do their best work. Whatever the reason, *Camille* is her masterpiece.

MARRIAGE, ITALIAN STYLE

Sophia Loren was a sex symbol first and an actress second, but what a sex symbol! Growing up poor in Naples, she first became known in beauty contests when she was young. Then she moved onto films, where her career was in budding form when she met producer Carlo Ponti, who became her mentor and later her husband. With her almond-shaped eyes, full lips, and almost supernaturally proportioned figure, Loren quickly emerged as an object of affection for men all over the world.

Marriage, Italian Style was based on playwright Eduardo De Filippo's *Filumena Maturano*. The role of Filumena, an Italian prostitute who suffers through the years at the hands of a typically chauvinist man named Domenico (Marcello Mastroianni), was a tour-de-force for the actress, allowing her to play a character who grows from girlhood to middle age against the changing landscape of postwar Italy.

What Loren lacked in subtlety she made up for with drive and charisma, in addition to her ripe beauty. Filumena is a true salt-of-the-earth peasant, unable to read but in possession of a big heart and common sense. Loren's best scenes in the role were those in which Filumena visits with her illegitimate sons, who are being raised by other families. These tender moments allowed her to project a bountiful motherly love that rang true in any language.

Since Loren's heyday in the 1950s and 1960s, film appearances have been spotty (especially since the death of Vittorio De Sica, who directed her Oscar-winning performance in 1960's *Two Women*). But she is still a symbol of great beauty and elegance.

> Marriage, Italian Style *offered Sophia Loren a tour-de-force opportunity in the role of Filumena, a salt-of-the-earth prostitute who grows from girlhood to middle age against the changing landscape of postwar Italy.*

> **Marriage, Italian Style**
> (1964)
> Screenplay by Renato Castellani, Tonia Guerra, Leo Benvenuti, and Piero de Bernardi, based on the play *Filumena Maturano* by Eduardo De Filippo
> Produced by Carlo Ponti
> Directed by Vittorio De Sica.
> (Embassy) 102 m.

❦ PATTON ❦

One of the most resonant movie images of the 1970s was that of George C. Scott as George S. Patton, World War II's greatest strategist and one of its most blustery, hard-nosed, colorful figures, striding before a gigantic American flag and delivering a give-'em-hell speech to his unseen troops. At the time, outrage at the American involvement in Vietnam and militarism in general was at its peak, making the image a loaded and provocative one. But ironically, *Patton* was claimed by hawks and doves alike. It was the favorite film of then-president Richard Nixon, for instance, who saw it as a tribute to a great general, but it also affirmed for those in the antiwar movement—*and* the film's creators—just how megalomaniacal the military mind could be.

At the heart of the conflicting opinions over what Patton was and meant was George C. Scott's towering performance. His Patton was no dovish caricature (along the lines of his General Turgidson in 1964's *Dr. Strangelove*) but

neither was it a hawkish glorification. Scott caught the bravura, but he also caught the mania, the almost sadistic perfectionism of a brilliant demagogue who slapped a combat-fatigued private for what he considered cowardice and advocated attacking the Soviet Union, America's ally, at the end of World War II.

John Wayne badly wanted the role but more politically ambiguous actors were sought, including Burt Lancaster, Robert Mitchum, and Lee Marvin. In retrospect, it is difficult to imagine any of them attacking the role with Scott's thoroughness. He spent a considerable amount of time preparing, studying Patton in newsreels. He even used a false nose to look more like the patrician Virginia general. The result of his study showed in so many memorable moments, including that opening speech, the scene in which he warily links arms in a toast

> **Patton**
> **(1970)**
> Screenplay by Francis Ford Coppola and Edmund H. North. Produced by Frank McCarthy. Directed by Franklin J. Schaffner.
> (20th Century Fox) 171 m.

with a Russian general, and, of course, the scene in which he slaps the hospitalized soldier with maniacal fervor.

When he won an Oscar

for his portrayal, he showed an iconoclasm to match Patton's own by refusing the award, referring to the Oscar competition as a "meat market."

Decked out in full regalia including a riding crop and a pearl-handled revolver, George C. Scott as Gen. George S. Patton takes time out from his pressing military duties to pose for a portrait painter. Scott won an Oscar for his portrayal of the imperious World War II general in Patton.

In 1976, Sylvester Stallone was a young unknown who had played tiny roles in a few films, including Woody Allen's *Bananas* (1971) and *Farewell, My Lovely* (1975) (he even appeared in a soft-core porno flick, later redubbed *The Italian Stallion*). It was all the

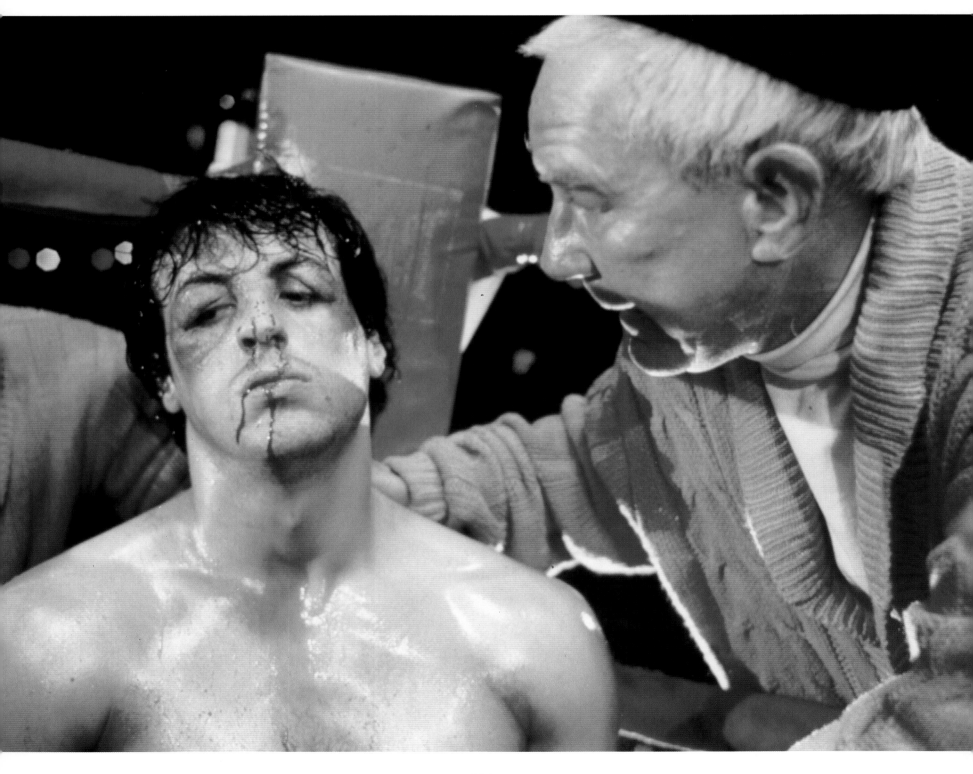

After the success of Rocky, *Sylvester Stallone found that audiences would not accept him in any other role. Then he played the muscle-bound killing machine, John Rambo, in* First Blood *(1982). He is seen here in the second of the Rambo films,* Rambo: First Blood Part II *(1985).*

OPPOSITE: *Seen here with Burgess Meredith as his manager is Sylvester Stallone, who became an instant star playing Rocky Balboa, the resilient, punch-drunk fighter who gets a Cinderella shot at the heavyweight championship of the world. The actor also scripted the Oscar-winning film,* Rocky.

more outrageous, then, that with no screen record to speak of he boldly walked into the office of producers Robert Chartoff and Irwin Winkler and convinced them to do a script that he had written about a down-and-out boxer from the Philadelphia streets who gets to fight the heavyweight champ, Apollo Creed (ultimately played by Carl Weathers). The rags to riches scenario played itself out both on-screen and off—the big dumb-looking guy took a percentage of the profits.

The first *Rocky* is a gritty, low-budget fairy tale, and Stallone's fighter is impossible not to love. He is not stupid, as wags have characterized him, but punchy, with a good sense of humor about himself. When he is offered the shot at the title as a publicity stunt, he doesn't kid himself into thinking he can win. He goes into the ring knowing that if he can just go the distance—something no one had ever done with Creed—he'll come out a winner. More importantly, he uses the title shot to get his life in order, quitting his job as a bone crusher for a local loan shark and managing to establish a wholesome relationship with Adrian (Talia Shire), the painfully shy sister of his best friend Paulie (Burt Young).

Stallone's secret as an actor lay in those big bassett hound eyes. While Al Pacino and Robert De Niro were busy putting the ethnic hero on the map with unvarnished realism and artistry, Stallone was doing his part with old-fashioned sentiment and heroism. At a time when movies were predominantly life-sized, Stallone's lowlife Cinderella story was a change of pace. The big shambling oaf in the porkpie hat and leather coat, speaking in that often-imitated baritone drawl, yelling the name of his beloved Adrian, was a strong dose of sugar in an era that was straight vinegar.

▶▶▶▶▶▶▶▶▶▶▶

Rocky
(1976)
Screenplay by Sylvester Stallone. Produced by Robert Chartoff, Irwin Winkler, and Gene Kirkwood. Directed by John G. Avildsen.
(United Artists) 119 m.

Given the fact that *It Happened One Night* is such a joyful and relaxed film, it comes as something of a shock to learn that its mak-

Margaret Sullavan for the role of Ellie Andrews, a runaway heiress who travels from Florida to New York with a reporter and falls for him along the way. But they were

far less prestigious studio than Gable's own, as a "punishment." But something must have gone right somewhere, because the film turned out to be delightful,

Forced to share a roadside motel room together, Ellie Andrews (Claudette Colbert) and Peter Warner (Clark Gable) improvise privacy by hanging up of a flimsy blanket to divide the room. Moviegoers everywhere were delighted when the "walls of Jericho" fell at the end of the picture.

becoming the prototype for the many screwball comedies that followed.

The magic in the pairing of Gable and Colbert came in part from their roles' inherently opposite qualities. Ellie is a spoiled rich girl whom Peter calls "Brat," putting her on a budget and watching over her like a mother hen. Peter is the "working Joe" incarnate, who considers dunking donuts and hitchhiking major art forms. Initially, Ellie responds to him like a

It Happened One Night
(1934)
Screenplay by Robert Riskin, based on the story "Night Bus" by Samuel Hopkins. Produced by Harry Cohn. Directed by Frank Capra.
(Columbia) 105 m.

ing was not an entirely happy experience. Director Frank Capra wanted a proven light comedienne like Miriam Hopkins or

unavailable and he had to settle for Claudette Colbert, who initially disliked Capra as a director (she also initially refused to expose her leg for the famous hitchhiking scene). And Clark Gable had no great desire to play the role of the reporter. He was loaned by MGM to Columbia, a

ONE NIGHT

Proving that opposites attract, Clark Gable as a reporter with a "working Joe" mentality and Claudette Colbert as a runaway heiress fall in love on the road from Florida to New York, in the prototype of all screwball comedies, It Happened One Night.

petulant child but she finally becomes affectionate. And he eventually warms up to her. After all, she can hitchhike better than he can.

Gable played the role with his characteristic gruff charm, keying with particular effectiveness into the moments when Peter resists the attraction he feels for Ellie, like an older man hiding his feelings for a young girl. And

Colbert, poised and beautiful, expertly played a woman falling in love. There is a moment when her face is beautifully lit by moonlight, and Ellie looks at Peter with the most delicate mixture of sexual longing and childish innocence. The two of them make *It Happened One Night* a funny yet true portrait of opposites attracting. In a rare Hollywood coup, Gable, Colbert, Capra, writer Robert Riskin, and the film itself swept the Oscars in 1934.

Peter teaches Ellie the proper way to "dunk" in It Happened One Night. *Both actors won Oscars for their work on the film.*

Marlon Brando has become a larger-than-life figure, a mercurial character whose lifestyle befits the Olympian talent with which he was blessed. Indeed, he appears at times to

have passed beyond mere acting. In his youth, he revolutionized film acting by bringing a more intuitive, "method"-driven style to parts such as Stanley Kowalski in *A Streetcar Named Desire* (1951) and Terry Malloy in *On the Waterfront* (1954). Even in the tiny, multimillion dollar character roles with which his fans have had to be content for the last 20 years, his outsized talent has made itself felt. Perhaps if there were one late-career part that symbolized his towering presence in the movies, it was Vito Corleone, the all-powerful patriarch and title character of *The Godfather*.

The godfather is a wise Mafia chieftain who has earned the respect of all the other crime "families" in New York through his careful exercise of terror, epitomized by his understated willingness to make people offers that they can't refuse. Beginning with the long opening sequence,

Brando revolutionized film acting with roles such as Terry Malloy, the ex-fighter who informs on the mob that controls the longshoremen unions in On the Waterfront *(1954). In this scene, he delivers the famous "I coulda been a contender" speech to his brother, Charlie (Rod Steiger).*

in which the godfather listens to supplicants' requests for "extra-legal help" in matters ranging from immigration difficulties to murder, Brando endowed the character with a regal authority that never diminishes, not even in Don Corleone's dotage. He found a slow way of moving and speaking, which suggested that this godfather didn't have

Brando offered a picture of alienation in The Wild One *(1954), inspiring the rebellious youngsters of an otherwise conformist decade. This shot of him in black-leather motorcycle regalia became an icon.*

to wait or rush for anyone, and that quality made Vito Corleone appear monumental. Originally the script called for a scene in which the godfather visits his dying consigliere, Genco, in the hospital. Genco asks him to send death away, since he is the godfather and has the power. The scene was eventually cut, perhaps because it was not needed. The power was implicit in Brando's portrayal.

The actor won his second Oscar for the role that was almost played by Laurence Olivier (writer Mario Puzo wanted Brando). Long an advocate of Native American rights, he sent an emissary named Sasheen Littlefeather to turn it down.

The Godfather
(1972)
Screenplay by Francis Ford Coppola and Mario Puzo, based on the novel by Puzo. Produced by Albert S. Ruddy. Directed by Francis Ford Coppola.

(Paramount) 175 m.

RIGHT: *Marlon Brando was a young, Actor's Studio-trained rebel when he re-created his Broadway triumph as Stanley Kowalski in the 1951 screen adaptation of Tennessee Williams'* A Streetcar Named Desire.

BELOW: *Brando, in his Oscar-winning performance as Don Vito Corleone, hears a murderous request from a friend in* The Godfather.

There were movie stars before Rudolph Valentino, but he was the first superstar. Rodolpho Guglielmi di Valentina d'Antonguolla had legions of adoring fans and detractors: he was alternately known as "the Great Lover" and "the Pink Powderpuff." He began as a tango dancer and worked his way into films on the strength of his extraordinary looks.

Valentino's most popular vehicle was *The Sheik,* in which he played a desert chieftain who captures from a band of English adventurers a young woman masquerading as an Arab (Agnes Ayres). Valentino maintained a sleek, outlandishly romantic intensity throughout the film, helping to make the sheik a figure of some note in the popular culture of the 1920s, and in-spiring, among other things, the popular song "The Sheik of Araby." One of the most memorable moments of the entire silent era came when the sheik scooped the yielding woman into his arms and carried her off to his tent (refined culture swept away by savage instinct, a popular theme of the period).

The Sheik
(1921)
Screenplay by Monte M. Katterjohn, based on the novel by E. M. Hull. Directed by George Melford. (Famous Players/Lasky) 73 m.

Valentino had just completed an even more popular sequel, *The Son of the Sheik* (1926) when at the age of 31 he died of complications from peritonitis. Some of the hoopla at his funeral—a mysterious lady veiled in black, a card with flowers supposedly "From Benito" (Mussolini, that is)—was faked by press agents. But the throngs of mourners who filled the streets and the fans who threatened or committed suicide on hearing of his death were real. Valentino was the first star to inspire such devotion.

Rudolph Valentino's most sensational role was that of a dashing Arab chieftain in The Sheik.

The three light comedies that Rock Hudson and Doris Day made together in the late 1950s and early 1960s have come to symbolize another era, the age before such issues as women's liberation and safe sex radically changed relationships between men and women. With their light, stylish byplay, their plush sets, and their fluffy romantic complications, the Day–Hudson pairings eschewed conviction in favor of effervescent fun, executed with great skill and care.

>>>>>>>>>>>>>

Pillow Talk
(1959)
Screenplay by Stanley Shapiro and Maurice Richlin, based on a story by Russell Rouse and Clarence Greene. Produced by Ross Hunter and Martin Melcher. Directed by Michael Gordon.
(Universal) 110 m.

In *Pillow Talk,* their first and best-remembered film, Hudson was Brad, a playboy composer who shares a party line with Day's Jan (even the names are redolent of another time). They despise one another sight unseen for bursting in on each other's telephone conversations, but Brad's interest is piqued when he finally glimpses Jan. Thereafter, he masquerades as a charming Southerner to win her over. Hudson was a Universal contract star who had made his name in a series of costume epics and "women's films" (including *Magnificent Obsession* with Jane Wyman). He was unsure of his ability to do comedy, but it proved to be his métier. His cheerful calm was a marvelous counterpoint to Day's end-of-the-tether nervousness. She was the prototypical working girl looking for the perfect mate and he was the model of the careless American playboy. Of course, no one was like them in real life. Just look at Day's wardrobe: no working girl ever dressed like that. Day and Hudson, along with their co-star Tony Randall, became great friends. The trio made two more films together of similar ilk: *Lover Come Back* (1961) and *Send Me No Flowers* (1964).

During the late 1950s and early 1960s Rock Hudson represented for millions of moviegoers the ideal man—handsome, personable, aggressive at work, and a hit with the ladies—and Doris Day the ideal woman—pretty, pert, and holding down a job but only until the right fellow comes along. The first of their three pairings, Pillow Talk was generally considered their best.

⟨⟩ SOPHIE'S CHOICE ⟨⟩

After a decade as a film star, Meryl Streep has established herself as the epitome of acting excellence, garnering Oscar nominations the way other people collect stamps. And perhaps no other actress of her generation has proven to be so versatile. For many, recognition of Streep's considerable talents initially came in the 1982 adaptation of William Styron's bestselling novel, *Sophie's Choice.*

Streep had distinguished herself in a number of supporting roles, particularly *The Deer Hunter* (1978) and *The Seduction of Joe Tynan* (1979), before tackling the role of Sophie Zowastowska, a Polish holocaust survivor. She was initially resistant to the part but then fought for it. And once she got it, she attacked it with her characteristic thoroughness and attention to detail. Even when she was not filming, she spoke in her immaculate Polish accent.

Styron's Sophie is a complex character—sweet, sexually volatile, holding onto life by

> ▶▶▶▶▶▶▶▶
> **Sophie's Choice**
> (1982)
> Screenplay by Alan J. Pakula. Produced by Keith Barish. Directed by Alan J. Pakula.
> (Universal) 157 m.
> ⸻

LEFT: *In the adaptation of John Fowles'* The French Lieutenant's Woman *(1981) Streep demonstrated her versatility in a dual role—that of a Victorian woman of mystery and the present-day actress who plays her on film.*

ABOVE: *Streep gave a performance that was alternately touching and rousing as an actress who tries to emerge from the long shadows cast by her movie-star mother (Shirley MacLaine) in* Postcards from the Edge *(1990), an adaptation of actress Carrie Fisher's autobiographical novel.*

ABOVE: *Meryl Streep won an Oscar for her performance as the tragic Sophie Zawostowska, a holocaust victim who lives in 1940s Brooklyn with her mad lover (Kevin Kline) in* Sophie's Choice.

her fingertips, in love with Nathan, a man she knows to be psychotic (Kevin Kline). Streep brought a deep vulnerability to the role, introducing, for example, a trembling quaver in So-

phie's voice that is like an open wound. She also brought an unusual, captivating beauty for, Streep's frequent protestations to the contrary, she was and is an exquisite camera subject, a hypnotic presence. Ultimately, she dominated *Sophie's Choice* in a way that few actresses have ever dominated a film, winning an Oscar as a consequence. Every moment, every word, every hesitation of Streep's Sophie is preparation for the convulsive moment in flashback where she must make the monstrous choice forced upon her by a Nazi officer.

ELMER GANTRY

Burt Lancaster conveys power on the screen. He has the physique of an athlete, which is matched by an actor's instinct for sharp

1946 debut, or *Crimson Cross* (1948), his physical presence had to be toned down to suit the doomed heroes he played. And in his later years, he muted

more control over the roles he played, he struck a particularly rich vein in his career, creating a series of flamboyant, highly charged characters, beginning

The energy, the sheer physical exuberance that Burt Lancaster brought to his Oscar-winning performance in the title role of Elmer Gantry, *comes through loud and clear in this photo of a 1920s religious revival meeting.*

physicality. This awareness even extends to his on-screen speech: he bites into his words. In such *films noir* as *The Killers,* his

his power in films such as *Atlantic City* (1980) in favor of a warm, autumnal glow. But in the mid-1950s, when he had

with the 1952 swashbuckler, *The Crimson Pirate*. With *Elmer Gantry*, eight years later, he hit the motherlode: he gave

Lancaster had to tone down his intense physicality to play the doomed hero of Criss Cross *(1948). He is pictured here with his co-star, Yvonne De Carlo, who would later play Lily Munster on the popular television show* The Munsters.

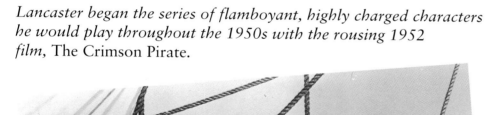

an Oscar-winning performance that nearly burst with energy.

Lancaster's Gantry is a 1920s traveling salesman who lives for the moment of the pitch but can't make a dollar. Despondent, he joins a travel-ing revivalist (Jean Simmons) and with his mesmerizing testimonies turns her middling tent-show success into a giant moneymaker. There was barely a moment in this performance when Lancaster wasn't smiling or letting his famous laugh fill the air, and he kept Elmer in almost constant, dynamic motion. But his evangelist is not simply a phony charlatan. Rather he is an essentially good man whose energies carry him away. The joy that he takes in lovemaking or in holding a crowd spellbound are one and the same. When, for example, Elmer has his first taste of success from the soapbox, Lancaster simply radiates excitement. For Elmer, Christianity is the greatest sell of all.

Lancaster began the series of flamboyant, highly charged characters he would play throughout the 1950s with the rousing 1952 film, The Crimson Pirate.

❦ SOME LIKE IT HOT ❦

As two musicians who witness the St. Valentine's Day Massacre, flee Chicago in drag disguises, and join an all-girl orchestra headed for Florida, Jack Lemmon and Tony Curtis look like they must have had a high time making *Some Like It Hot.* In reality, the filming was something of a nightmare thanks to a depressed Marilyn Monroe as the band's singer and the Curtis character's love interest. Her condition, which resulted in muffed lines and missed cues, forced director Billy Wilder to shoot

Some Like It Hot
(1959)
Screenplay by Billy Wilder and I. A. L. Diamond, suggested by a story by R. Thoeren and M. Logan. Produced and directed by Billy Wilder.
(United Artists) 122 m.

Tony Curtis (left) and Jack Lemmon are "Josephine" and "Daphne," a couple of girls on the run from the gang that committed the St. Valentine's Day Massacre, in Some Like It Hot.

so many takes of her scenes that Curtis, in particular, was miserable. But what went on backstage could not diminish the exuberance that the two lead actors projected on screen.

Lemmon was particularly hilarious as Jerry, pitched between bliss and exasperation, as he unthinkingly sinks deeper and deeper into the role of "Daphne" and her

romance with a millionaire (Joe E. Brown). Their courtship is complete with moonlight, champagne, and a diamond embedded between Daphne's teeth during a torrid tango. (Perhaps Lemmon's funniest scene, however, is that in which Daphne is surrounded by a throng of orchestra mates in their nightgowns aboard a train, and Jerry is almost delirious with happiness.)

Lemmon's ditsy behavior was well-balanced by Curtis' relative calm and self-confidence as Josephine. And one must applaud the very credible Cary Grant imitation that he employs in yet another disguise, that of an impotent millionaire, which he dons to woo Monroe's Sugar.

Lemmon and Curtis offered the most renowned drag act in movies, capped off by the immortal closing scene, written the night before it was shot, in which Jerry tells his/her suitor that they can't wed because he's a man, and Brown replies as only he can: "Nobody's perfect."

Producer David O. Selznick tried to turn the casting of the unnamed wife in his version of Daphne du

Maurier's *Rebecca* into as much of a media event as the search for Scarlett in *Gone With the Wind,* but the choice was never much in doubt. Director Alfred Hitchcock initially favored Margaret Sullavan, but he and Selznick were finally won over by Joan Fontaine (Olivia de Havilland was also considered, but she dropped out of the running because she didn't want to compete with her sister).

The special quality that Joan Fontaine brought to the screen—a mixture of girlish beauty, cultured bearing, and a constitution so delicate that it seemed she might break—limited her as an actress. But it was perfect for the role of Mrs. Maxim de Winter, the woman who marries a handsome British nobleman (Laurence Olivier) and tries to fill the shoes of his dead but all-powerful first wife, Rebecca. Fontaine was the very essence of a nervous, halting woman who, no matter what she does or where she goes, continues to be haunted by the spirit of her predecessor.

Ironically, hers was a situation that somewhat mirrored Fontaine's own during filming, for director Hitchcock exercised as firm a grip on the novice star as Rebecca did on the wife. And on top of that, her co-star spent much of the time grumbling about his lover, Vivien Leigh, not being cast in the role. Fontaine's scenes with Judith Anderson's Mrs. Danvers, the evil housekeeper who worships Rebecca, are the most memorable, with Anderson's black eyes seeming to burn holes in Fontaine's pure soul.

Joan Fontaine won an Oscar for her performance as the nameless heroine of Rebecca, *seen here under the spell of evil housekeeper Mrs. Danvers (Judith Anderson, right).*

Although he parlayed his talents and reputation to mega-star status in the 1980s with a series of outlandish character roles, Jack Nicholson was throughout the 1970s, the actor who best represented the angry fringe of American society: bored, disillusioned, having no particular place to go, and belonging to nothing and no one. From *Easy Rider* (1969) to *The Passenger* (1975), Nicholson was not quite a star but an actor who starred in offbeat, fascinating films, embodying sentiments that did not surface in the majority of Hollywood's output.

The situation changed dramatically with *One Flew Over the Cuckoo's Nest*. Not only did this film earn him his first Oscar, it made him a superstar. For the role of McMurphy, the wild free spirit who battles the authoritarian nurse Ratched (Louise Fletcher) for the souls of his fellow inmates at an Oregon mental institution, Nicholson spent many hours observing patients in the hospital in which the film was shot. He watched them receiving shock treatments, mingled with them in the recreation room, and slept at the facility with the rest of the cast throughout the filming. The result was more than worth the effort.

As opposed to the macho Mc-

Nicholson took his angry persona and pushed it to outrageous extremes in director Stanley Kubrick's adaptation of Stephen King's The Shining *(1980). In this moment—one of the most famous of the decade—he perversely exclaims, "Here's Johnny!" as he breaks down the door to the bathroom in which his wife is hiding.*

LEFT: *In* Batman *(1989), Nicholson stole the show as the Joker, one of several outlandish character roles he played during the 1980s.*

ABOVE: *After his memorable supporting role in* Easy Rider *(1969), Nicholson established himself as a star in* Five Easy Pieces *(1970), playing a rebel from a cultured musical family who chooses to wear a hardhat and bed an unsophisticated but good-hearted woman, played by Karen Black.*

LEFT: *Not only did the role of McMurphy in* One Flew Over the Cuckoo's Nest *earn Jack Nicholson his first Oscar, it made him a superstar. The actor spent hours observing mental patients to prepare for the part of the free-spirited hospital inmate.*

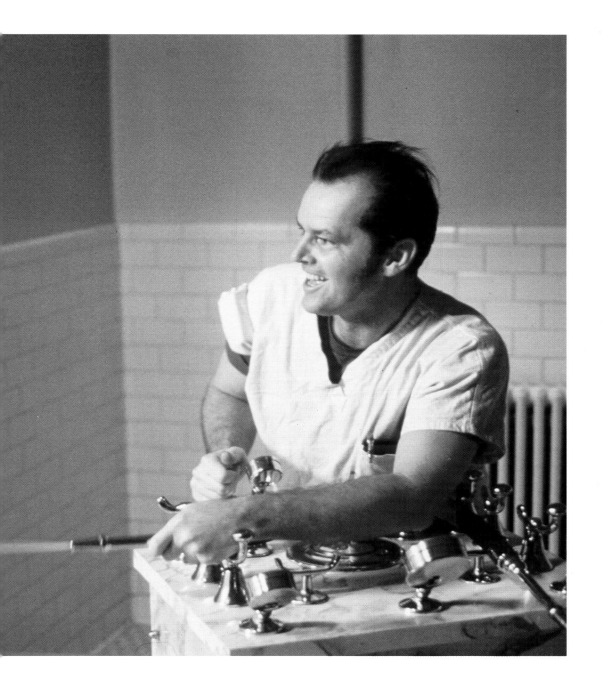

Murphy of Ken Kesey's novel, written in the 1950s, Nicholson played the character as a gentle-spirited, more introspective drifter. It gave him a golden opportunity to showcase his unique gifts: his ability to explode with manic energy, his charm (always with a hint of deviousness), and his famous, sunburst grin, which prompted *Time* magazine to call its 1974 cover story on him "The Star with the Killer Smile."

One Flew Over the Cuckoo's Nest
(1975)

Screenplay by Lawrence Hauben and Bo Goldman, based on the novel by Ken Kesey. Produced by Saul Zaentz and Michael Douglas. Directed by Milos Forman.

(United Artists) 134 m.

William Powell, he of the angular chin and the dry wit, emerged as a star in the silent era. So did Myrna Loy, who specialized in Asian temptresses. But it was with the coming of sound and in tandem that they made an impact. They were initially cast together in *Manhattan Melodrama* (1934), and director W. S. Van Dyke thought that they worked so well together he quickly cast them in his adaptation of Dashiell Hammett's murder mystery, *The Thin Man*. Powell and Loy went on to do five more *Thin Man* films together in addition to many other screwball comedies throughout the 1930s, notably *Libeled Lady* (1936).

Powell had already played a debonair urbanite detective in the four films of the Philo Vance series from 1929 to 1933. But his pairing with Loy upped the ante. Her Nora was a sort of gorgeous straight man to Powell's Nick, around to mix the ever-flowing supply of martinis and match her spouse in humor equally as dry. In the midst of the Depression, they were the embodiment of freedom from worry and care, with Nick forever lazing around, prodded by Nora to dive into the excitement of solving a good murder. One of the most charming moments in the series has Nick idly snuffing out Christmas tree balls with an air pistol he's gotten as a present, while Nora, wrapped in a fur,

The Thin Man
(1934)
Screenplay by Frances Goodrich and Albert Hackett, based on the novel by Dashiell Hammett. Produced by Hunt Stromberg. Directed by W. S. Van Dyke.
(MGM) 93 m.

watches with amusement. To appreciate how well Powell and Loy worked together, one need only watch *Star of Midnight* (1935), a *Thin Man* duplicate with Powell playing Nick Charles in all but name and Ginger Rogers playing the Nora role. It is a perfectly pleasant film and there was nothing wrong with the pairing, but

Powell and Loy were often teamed together outside of the Thin Man *series. They are pictured here as legendary showman Florenz Ziegfeld and actress Billie Burke in* The Great Ziegfeld *(1936).*

MAN

there was no chemistry between them. Perhaps what made the Powell and Loy team work so well was that Nick and Nora's adoration for one another seemed to be a given beneath all their urbane sophistication. They never had to show it, and therefore the actors' films soared.

Depression-era audiences found welcome relief from life's realities in the adventures of Nick and Nora Charles (William Powell and Myrna Loy), a wealthy, urbane couple that dabbled in detective work. They are shown here with their dog "Asta" in The Thin Man, *the first in the series of six entertaining films.*

Since the late 1960s, the role of the kind but tough teacher, whose care for his or her students takes the form of gruffness and high expectations, has been seen repeatedly in movies and television shows. The film that started the trend was *To Sir, with Love*. As dated and schematic as some of the film seems 25 years later, it remains affecting due to the presence and talent of Sidney Poitier in the role of Mark Thackery, or "Sir," as his students call him. Ironically, 12 years earlier Poitier had played a delinquent in *The Blackboard Jungle* (1955).

Mark is an engineer from British Guiana who, to make ends

>>>>>>>>>>>>>>
To Sir, with Love
(1967)
Screenplay by James Clavell, based on the novel by E. R. Braithwaite. Produced and directed by James Clavell.
(Columbia) 105 m.
⸺ ▪ ⸺

unruly students (two of whom are played by Judy Geeson and pop singer Lulu, who rendered the hit title song) until he decides to stop teaching the three Rs and start preparing the young adults for life.

What Poitier brought to this role was a deep sense of humility, caring, and pride. Although Mark is not confident about every move and decision he makes, he has good instincts, and in time he learns to trust them. He is also a striking figure of a man—handsome, strong, vigorous. The girl students fall in love with him, and the boy students want to be like him.

Poitier seemed to radiate love in most of his film roles but never more so than when he played Sir. At the film's end, when his graduating students present him with a gift, he is so moved that, rather than betray his emotion, he strides out of the room with the greatest dignity. It is easy to imagine other actors wallowing in the pathos of the moment, but Poitier plays against it and is all the more affecting for that.

As part of his effort to teach his students about life, "Sir" (Sidney Poitier) demonstrates the proper way to make a salad in To Sir, with Love.

meet, takes an interim job as a teacher in a London school for delinquent adolescents. Along with the school's other instructors, he has a hard time with his

Jean-Paul Belmondo is widely regarded as the French Bogart: not handsome in any classical way but sexy, cocky, and at the same time, world-weary. But unlike Bogart, there is a bit of the clown about Belmondo, a sense that he is fate's fool. He was a young actor who had played dozens of small parts in films when he was chosen by director Jean-Luc Godard for his revolutionary first feature, *Breathless, or A Bout de Souffle.* Godard saw in the action that mixture of the antic and the tragic, and put him in the role that would define him throughout his career.

Breathless, the story goes, was shot without sound on rolls of 35-millimeter still-camera film that had been taped together, giving the result a spontaneity and freshness that would make it the signal movie of the French New Wave (the dia-logue was dubbed in later). But, while breaking new ground, Godard and Belmondo also paid homage to the American cinema of the past. At one point in *Breathless,* Poiccard stands next to a poster of Bogart, imitates the actor's gesture of rubbing his lower lip with his thumb, and murmurs the name "Bogie" with religious awe. It's a charming moment and one that informs the whole performance. The gangly Poiccard, on the lam with his girlfriend (Jean Seberg) after accidentally killing a cop during a heist, never seems to be a serious hood—he's just playing cops and robbers. Likewise, *Breathless* is no taut thriller, but a philosophical inquiry, a tribute to American movies, an appreciation of Paris. After the film's release, Belmondo's Poiccard became a new kind of hero in a new kind of movie: self-aware, intellectual, stylized, and bitterly romantic. With his gravelly voice and boxer's pug nose, the French actor projected an anarchistic charm that perfectly anticipated the mood of the 1960s.

> **Breathless, or A Bout de Souffle**
> (1959)
> Script by Jean-Luc Godard, based on an idea by Francois Truffaut. Produced by Georges de Beauregard. Directed by Jean-Luc Godard.
> (Films Around the World) 90 m.

Jean-Paul Belmondo created a new kind of movie hero as Michel Poiccard, the petty thief of Breathless, *seen here strolling through Paris with his American girlfriend Marlon (Jean Seberg).*

Marlene Dietrich liked to claim that her film career began in 1930 with *The Blue Angel* and in many ways she was right. Although she had made several films in Germany during the 1920s, she hadn't become a significant presence in movies until she became associated with director Josef Von Sternberg, who made *Angel* in Germany and then took his star to America where they made six more striking, outlandishly stylized films together over the next five years.

Whether or not Sternberg was Dietrich's Svengali is open to debate. The actress herself seemed to endorse such a notion throughout her career. But in his autobiography, the great director claimed to

Marlene Dietrich was the last word in glamor as Shanghai Lily, the temptress of the east, admired here by her former lover Captain Harvey (Clive Brook) in Josef Von Sternberg's Shanghai Express.

Shanghai Express
(1932)
Screenplay by Jules
Furthman. Directed by
Josef Von Sternberg.
(Paramount) 84 m.

*Dietrich is seen
here during the
later phase of her
career in director
Billy Wilder's
adaptation of
Agatha Christie's*
Witness for the
Prosecution
(1957).

be embarrassed by the role attributed to him. On the other hand, he indicated in the same work that he gave his star such directions as, "Drop your voice an octave and don't lisp," and, "Count to six and look at that lamp as if you could no longer live without it." While it is true that their seven collaborations produced what might be called "director's films," it is also fair to say that Dietrich was striking in them.

"It took more than one man to call me Shanghai Lil," says Dietrich's character early on in *Shanghai Express*, perhaps the most famous film of the series. Her characterization of a scarlet woman with a heart of gold, ready to sacrifice all for the man she loves (Clive Brook), was made of measured furtive glances, short verbal exchanges delivered in the German actress' famous low, accented drawl, and dramatically shot close-ups of one of the movies' most beautiful faces. It may not have been great acting, but it was most certainly a thing of motion picture beauty. The fact is that Dietrich was not just a pretty face who photographed well: she was a creature of film.

Dietrich in one of her best post-Von Sternberg roles, as the saloon singer who is romanced by the local sheriff (James Stewart) in Destry Rides Again *(1939).*

Dustin Hoffman as Benjamin Braddock

Released in 1967, *The Graduate* was the first movie to catch the alienated mood of American youth in the turbulent 1960s. For all its stylistic bravura, Dustin Hoffman's Benjamin instead of seeking a career in plastics—as one of his father's friends suggests—he drifts into a meaningless affair with an older woman, Mrs. Robinson (Anne Bancroft). Here was a seed of revolt, reflected in a quietly numb

After The Graduate, *Hoffman scored another triumph as Ratso Rizzo, the down-and-out New York street hustler who befriends a would-be Texas stud named Joe Buck (Jon Voight) in* Midnight Cowboy *(1969).*

Ironically, Hoffman felt that he was completely wrong for the role that made his career, and, from the description of the character in the novel, he was right. He was, as he saw it, too ethnic, too short, and not handsome enough for the role. But director Mike Nichols held out. He knew that the latent aggressiveness beneath Hoffman's good-boy facade was what the part demanded. When Benjamin finally takes action at the end of the film and rescues Mrs. Robinson's daughter Elaine (Katharine Ross), with whom he

Braddock was the key to the film's success. As a new Ivy League graduate returning to his California home, dressed in the WASP uniform of oxford shirt, sport jacket, and loafers, Benjamin embodied the youthful middle class at that time. But, dissatisfaction. Benjamin reflects a generation's bewilderment and disgust at the middle-class hypocrisies of their parents. It is not difficult to imagine Benjamin metamorphosing from here into one of the hippie bikers in *Easy Rider* (1969).

For the title role in Hook *(1991), director Steven Spielberg's sequel to* Peter Pan, *Hoffman based his portrayal on Britain's King Charles II and on America's political commentator William F. Buckley!*

LEFT: *In* Tootsie *(1982), Dustin Hoffman was hilarious—and convincing—as Dorothy Michaels, the overnight sensation of a daytime soap. Hoffman's Michael Dorsey dons the disguise when he finds that no one will hire him as an actor.*

BELOW: *Dustin Hoffman became a star in his first film role, that of the alienated Benjamin Braddock in* The Graduate. *Here, in one of the movie's most famous moments, the honors student receives a one-word piece of advice from a family friend—"plastics."*

The Graduate
(1967)
Screenplay by Calder Willingham and Buck Henry, based on the novel by Charles Webb. Produced by Lawrence Turman. Directed by Mike Nichols.
(Embassy) 105 m.

has fallen in love, from a conventional marriage, it is, at first, a great catharsis. But as he and Elaine ride away together on a bus, Hoffman's blank, alienated stare leaves the audience wondering where the pair will be in a few years. It is a look that reflected well a nation in transition.

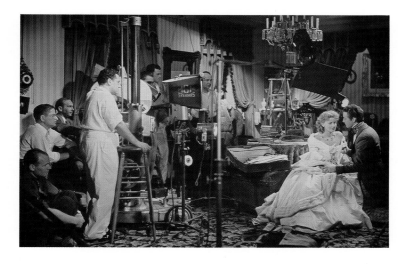

☙ ACKNOWLEDGEMENTS ❧

The producers of this book gratefully acknowledge the efforts of the following motion picture studios, whose dedication to high-quality entertainment has enriched the lives of moviegoers everywhere: Allied Artists, American International Pictures, Avco Embassy, Columbia Pictures, First Artists, Lucasfilm, Metro-Goldwyn-Mayer, Orion Pictures, Paramount Pictures, Republic Pictures, RKO, Tri-Star Pictures, 20th Century Fox, United Artists, Universal Studios, Walt Disney Studios, Warner Brothers.

☙ INDEX TO THE ACTORS ❧

ABOVE: *The making of* Camille *starring Greta Garbo as the fading but still luminous Marguerite Gautier. With her here is co-star Robert Taylor as Armand. Director George Cukor is standing at left.*